MILLIONAIRES OFFSHORE

BLUEPRINT TO SUCCESS

Akinwumi Oyadola Dosumu

CONTENTS

D e d i c a t i o n

This book is dedicated to the visionaries who have charted their own course through the unpredictable seas of life. To Diamond Oluwatoyin Dosumu, Matthias Akinyele Dosumu, Grace Yetunde Dosumu, Olumide Sunday Dosumu, Dr. Oko Obasi, Akinwunmi Oyedola Dosumu, Seun Oluwaseun Dosumu, Ayomide Grace Dosumu, and Barr. Temitope Dosumu esq.

Your stories illuminate the pages of "Millionaires Offshore," serving as guiding stars for those navigating their personal journeys. May your achievements inspire others to set sail into the vast ocean of possibilities and discover the treasures that await on their own unique voyages.

Acknowledgments

I wish to extend my heartfelt gratitude to the Almighty God, the guiding force behind every odyssey. To you, the cherished reader, who embarked on this journey, thank you for allowing these stories to set sail in your imagination.

Special appreciation is extended to Dr. Oko Obasi, a compass of wisdom and inspiration. To my parents, whose support has been an anchor through turbulent times, and to every individual who has played a significant role in shaping this narrative—your contributions are deeply valued.

With love and appreciation,

Akinwumi Oyedola Dosumu
Abuja,Nigeria
January,2024

PREFACE

In the vast expanse of life's ocean, we are all sailors, navigating the turbulent seas of challenges and uncertainties. "Millionaires Offshore: Blueprint of Success" is an exploration of the remarkable stories of individuals who not only weathered the storms but also found prosperity on distant shores.

Welcome aboard the captivating journey of "Millionaires Offshore" In the vast sea of personal and financial success, this book serves as your compass, guiding you through uncharted waters and revealing the hidden treasures that await those who dare to chart their own course.

Life, much like the turbulent seas, presents us with challenges and uncertainties. It is in these moments of adversity that we often discover our true strength and resilience. In the chapters that follow, we will dive deep into personal stories of struggle and triumph, learning invaluable lessons from the school of hard knocks.

But this book is not just about overcoming obstacles; it's about setting sail in search of a North Star. We will embark on a journey to define success on our own terms, identifying personal goals that resonate with our deepest desires. Together, we will craft a vision for the future, a compass that will guide us through the choppy waters of life.

As you embark on this journey, you'll encounter tales of early struggles, resilience in the face of adversity, and the invaluable lessons learned in the school of hard knocks. Each chapter unfolds like a nautical chart, guiding you through the uncharted waters of personal growth, wealth-building strategies, and the global landscape of success.

This book is not just about financial triumph; it's a compass that points towards a life well-lived. Through the stories of those who dared to cast off into the unknown, you will discover the art of vision, the science of resilience, and the wisdom of navigating the complex currents of the business world.

Our exploration takes us beyond borders, showcasing international success stories and the opportunities that lie in offshore ventures. We delve into the strategies of those who have sailed through economic downturns and embraced the challenges of the global market. "Millionaires Offshore" is not a mere collection of success stories; it's a guide for you to chart your own course. It invites you to cast off the anchors that hold you back, set sail towards your dreams, and navigate towards a future filled with prosperity.

As we weather the storms that inevitably come our way, we will explore strategies for resilience and perseverance. By sharing stories of those who have overcome setbacks, we will discover the power of staying afloat even in the most challenging times. And when opportunities arise, we will learn to spot hidden gems in the business world, nurturing the entrepreneurial spirit within us.

In the pursuit of wealth and prosperity, we will delve into wealth-building strategies, exploring investments and financial planning as anchors to secure our future. We will also venture into the realm of offshore opportunities, where the vast potential for growth awaits those who dare to harness it.

But this voyage is not confined to a single land. We will broaden our horizons and set sail towards international success stories, discovering how individuals have found their fortune abroad. By embracing global perspectives, we can expand our own personal growth and unlock new opportunities for success.

As we navigate the ever-changing economic landscape, we will learn to adapt to market changes and draw wisdom from past economic downturns. Charting the global landscape, we will explore cross-border opportunities, navigating legal and cultural challenges while forging valuable connections across borders.

In the midst of this grand adventure, we will also explore the hidden compass within us — our intuition and decision-making. By trusting our instincts and making sound choices, we can navigate the business world with confidence and purpose.

No journey is without its obstacles, and we will confront the barriers that stand in our way. From societal and gender challenges to pioneering new paths, we will draw inspiration from those who have broken free from the constraints of convention and blazed their own trails to success. Diversifying our investments, we will learn to balance risk and reward, building a robust portfolio that withstands the test of time. And as we accumulate wealth, we will discover the power of creating a lasting impact, balancing our success with social responsibility through philanthropy and giving back.

In the age of innovation, we will raise the sails of entrepreneurship, exploring case studies in business innovation and adapting to technological advancements. And as we approach calm waters and sunset dreams, we will uncover the secrets to achieving financial freedom, preserving our wealth, and savoring the fruits of our success. May the pages that follow inspire you to hoist your own sails, weather your personal storms, and discover the hidden treasures that await in the vast sea of opportunities.

As we reach the final pages of this voyage, take a moment to reflect on the lessons learned and the experiences shared. "Millionaires Offshore" is not just a book; it is an invitation to embark on your own remarkable journey. Whether you're an ambitious entrepreneur, a seasoned investor, or simply someone seeking personal growth, this book offers insights, inspiration, and encouragement to chart your own course to success.

Now, it is time to cast off, set sail, and explore the wealth of wisdom that awaits within the pages of "Millionaires Offshore." May this journey be transformative, empowering you to navigate the seas of life with confidence, purpose, and the determination to make your dreams a reality. Bon voyage!

Akinwumi Oyedola Dosumu
Abuja, Nigeria
January, 2024

CHAPTER 1

CASTING OFF

"The only way to do great work is to love what you do."

– Steve Jobs

The sun dipped low on the horizon, casting a warm glow across the restless waves as I stood on the shore, my gaze fixed on the vastness of the ocean. This was no ordinary evening; it was the commencement of a journey, an odyssey into the unknown, and the opening chapter of my narrative in "Millionaires Offshore."

As I inhaled the salty breeze, memories of countless stories flooded my mind – tales of those who, like me, had dared to cast off their anchors and set sail into the tumultuous yet exhilarating waters of life. Each story, a testament to the transformative power of resilience, determination, and the audacity to dream beyond the familiar shores.

In the quiet harbor of our lives, every individual's journey begins with the daunting task of casting off from the safety of the known shores into the vast and unpredictable sea of existence. This chapter sets sail with the stories of those who faced early struggles, a formidable initiation into the turbulent seas of life.

The timeless words of Oprah Winfrey resonated in me "The biggest adventure you can take is to live the life of your dreams."

So allow me to take you back to the moment when I first set foot on this path, when uncertainty loomed like a distant storm on the horizon. In the early days, the shore I stood upon felt stable and secure, but it was a place of comfort that could also breed complacency. Life, however, had other plans.

I vividly recall the struggles, the doubts, and the triumphs that marked my journey. Each challenge, a wave crashing against the hull of my aspirations, and each triumph, a gentle breeze filling the sails of my ambition. The undulating tides of life sculpted me into the person standing on this shore today, ready to share the wisdom gleaned from navigating the thousand waves.

Section A: Early Struggles

My own story echoes with reflections on personal growth, the forging of resilience in the crucible of challenges, and the realization that sometimes, the most remarkable destinations are reached through the roughest seas. We are confronted with the reality that as Mark Twain opined "Twenty years from now, you will be more disappointed by the things you didn't do than by the ones you did."

The sea, in all its majestic chaos, became a metaphor for life itself. Its unpredictable currents, the challenges we face, and its undulating waves, the highs and lows of our journey.

Navigating these waters requires learning to read the signs in the wind and understanding the language of the sea.

In this introductory chapter, we embark on a journey towards financial success as we explore the analogy of the knitting technique "Casting Off" and its application to the book "Millionaires Offshore: Blueprint of Success." We set sail with the intention of finishing strong, creating a solid foundation, tailoring strategies, and embracing the exciting adventure of wealth creation.

1. Finishing Strong
Just as casting off in knitting involves finishing the last row of stitches to create a neat and secure edge, our journey towards financial success begins with the understanding that finishing strong is crucial. We delve into the importance of starting well and ending well, ensuring that the efforts and achievements we make along the way are solidified and resilient.

2. Creating a Neat Edge
Similar to how casting off in knitting creates a neat edge that prevents the work from unraveling, the book "Millionaires Offshore" provides readers with a blueprint for success, guiding them in creating a solid foundation and structure for their financial endeavors. We explore practical strategies, insights, and techniques that help establish a strong financial position and protect wealth from potential risks.

3. Tailoring the Technique
Just as there are different methods of casting off in knitting, we acknowledge that each individual has unique goals, circumstances, and preferences when it comes to achieving financial success. The book recognizes the importance of tailoring strategies and approaches to suit individual needs

and aspirations. We present a range of options, empowering readers to find an approach that resonates with them and aligns with their personal situation.

4. Embracing Exciting Adventures
The analogy of casting off highlights the thrilling adventure of venturing into offshore opportunities and exploring the world of wealth creation. We encourage readers to embrace this journey, just as knitting offers a creative and fulfilling process. We delve into the excitement of building wealth offshore, discovering new avenues for financial growth, and expanding horizons beyond conventional boundaries.

Life, like the capricious waves, has a way of testing our mettle from the outset. Through personal narratives and shared experiences, we explore the adversities that early sailors encountered. These are tales of resilience, where individuals confronted challenges that shaped them into the captains of their destinies. From financial setbacks to personal tribulations, these stories lay the foundation for the profound lessons learned in the relentless school of hard knocks.

Section B: Lessons Learned in the School of Hard Knocks

In the crucible of adversity, valuable lessons are forged. This section delves into the wisdom gained from facing hardships head-on. These lessons are not just about survival but about thriving amidst the storm. From resilience and perseverance to the art of bouncing back stronger, we unravel the secrets that transform setbacks into stepping stones towards success.

I invite you to reflect on your own shores, the safe harbors you've grown accustomed to, and the comfort zones that, while familiar, might be limiting your potential. Let's ponder the beauty of embracing the unknown together, for it is only when we release ourselves from the moorings of fear, doubt, and societal expectations that we truly begin to create.

As we navigate the choppy waters of this chapter, it becomes evident that the process of casting off is not just a physical departure but a metaphorical shedding of self-doubt, fear, and limitations. These early struggles become the winds that propel the sail, setting the course for a journey where the destination is not just success but self-discovery and growth.

Oliver Goldsmith famous for the book "She Stoops to Conquer", a comedy of manners that satirizes the social and romantic pretensions of the upper class. Aptly expresses this assertion that "Life is a journey that must be travelled no matter how bad the roads and accommodations."

And so, my fellow voyager, the time has come to cast off. To set sail into the unknown, to navigate the unpredictable currents, and to discover the treasures hidden within the undulating tides. The shore is not the destination; it is the starting point of a grand adventure.

Let us embark on this odyssey of resilience, be guided by the timeless wisdom of Dorothy Thomas who said that "It is only when we are no longer fearful that we begin to create.". And so, our odyssey begins. The journey of a thousand waves has just started, and I am eager to share the unfolding narrative that lies ahead in the pages of "Millionaires Offshore." Where the act of casting off is not merely a departure but the first courageous step towards becoming a masterful navigator of life's unpredictable seas.

As we set sail into the first chapter of "Millionaires Offshore: Blueprint of Success," we establish the groundwork for our voyage. By applying the concept of casting off in knitting to the pursuit of financial success, we lay the foundation for finishing strong, creating a solid edge, tailoring strategies, and embracing the thrilling adventure that awaits. Let us embark on this voyage together, guided by the wisdom and insights that will shape our path to achieving financial abundance.

CHAPTER 2

IN SEARCH OF A NORTH STAR

"Success is not final, failure is not fatal: It is the courage to continue that counts."
– Winston Churchill

The concept of searching for a North Star serves as a powerful metaphor for discovering one's purpose, direction, or goal in life. Just as the North Star, or Polaris, remains a constant reference point in the sky for travelers and navigators, individuals use the idea of a North Star to guide their personal journey of self-discovery, growth, and the pursuit of meaning and fulfillment.

With the echoes of early struggles still resonating in the wind, our journey takes us deeper into the open sea of possibilities. Chapter Two unfolds as a compass, guiding individuals in search of their own North Star – a beacon of purpose and direction in the vast expanse of life. In the early days of my journey, the horizon seemed distant and shrouded in mist.

During this quest, individuals may engage in deep introspection and ask themselves thought-provoking questions such as:

- What are my core values, passions, and strengths?

- What dreams, aspirations, and visions do I hold?

- What gifts, talents, and skills do I possess?

- What roles, responsibilities, and relationships are important to me?

- What challenges, opportunities, and resources shape my path?

- What contributions, impacts, and legacies do I wish to create?

Through exploring these questions, individuals hope to uncover their own North Star, their true calling that inspires and motivates them, and aligns them with their highest potential. As I set sail into the uncharted waters of my ambitions, Chapter Two unfolds, a chapter not just about setting a course but about finding a guiding star in the vast expanse of possibilities. The sea, though boundless, can be navigated with purpose, and so can life.

The shores I had left behind were fading, and uncertainty loomed like a vast ocean stretching out before me. It was during this phase that the importance of finding a North Star became clear—a guiding light that would steer my ship through the darkness, providing direction in the midst of uncertainty.

Section A: Defining Success

Success is a destination, but the path to it is uniquely crafted by each sailor. In this section, we explore the diverse interpretations of success. I am reminded of an anecdote, a story that serves as a compass point in my own narrative. It was a time when doubt and indecision threatened to cast shadows over my journey. A mentor, a wise captain who had weathered storms before, shared a piece of wisdom that would resonate through the chapters of my life: "A ship without a North Star is at the mercy of the waves. Find your guiding light, and you will always find your way home."

The search for a North Star is not just about reaching a destination but about navigating the currents of life with purpose. This guiding light becomes a source of inspiration, a constant in the ever-changing sea of opportunities. Through personal anecdotes and reflections, individuals share their definitions, unveiling the multifaceted nature of achievement. From personal fulfillment to professional accomplishments, the concept of success is as diverse as the stars that guide us.

Section B: Identifying Personal Goals

The North Star serves as a celestial reference point for sailors, a constant in the night sky that provides guidance. Similarly, personal goals act as guiding lights in the journey of life. In the tumultuous sea of uncertainty, I found my North Star in the form of a clear vision. It was a vision that transcended mere financial success; it was a vision of impact, innovation, and leaving a lasting legacy. The North Star, in this context, was not just a destination but a principle—an unwavering commitment to a purpose-driven journey.

The chapter unfolds with reflections on the process of defining this North Star. It's not a one-size-fits-all beacon but a personal and profound realization of what truly matters. Akin to a sailor plotting the course, I delved into introspection, seeking clarity on my values, aspirations, and the legacy I wished to leave behind.

This section encourages readers to identify and articulate their aspirations, setting the stage for the chapters ahead. Whether it's financial independence, creative fulfillment, or meaningful relationships, the process of defining personal goals becomes a pivotal step in navigating the tumultuous waters.

Section C: Crafting a Vision for the Future

The narrative is enriched with anecdotes of individuals who, in their own quests, discovered their North Stars. These stories serve as beacons of inspiration, illuminating the myriad ways one can find purpose and direction in the vastness of life's oceans.

One such tale is that of an entrepreneur who, fueled by a passion for sustainability, forged a path toward environmentally conscious business practices. In this story, the North Star was not just a metaphor; it became a tangible commitment to contributing positively to the world.

As the chapter unfolds, the concept of the North Star expands beyond personal aspirations to encompass leadership. A true leader, much like a seasoned captain, is guided by a vision that transcends individual gain. The chapter shares stories of leaders who, by aligning their compass with a higher purpose, steered their organizations through turbulent waters to success.

A ship without a destination is adrift, and so is a life without a vision. We delve into the importance of crafting a clear vision for the future. Through inspirational stories and practical insights, this section encourages readers to visualize their desired destination and set a course for it. Crafting a vision becomes the compass that aligns actions with aspirations, steering individuals towards their North Star.

The search for a North Star is not a one-time endeavor; it's a continuous process of introspection and recalibration. Much like celestial navigation, it requires a keen awareness of one's position in the journey, an understanding of the changing tides, and the ability to adjust the sails accordingly.

The chapter serves not only as a guide for personal navigation but also as an invitation for readers to embark on their own quest for a North Star. It encourages introspection, asking the fundamental questions that illuminate the path forward. What values guide your journey? What legacy do you wish to leave behind? What is your North Star?

As I conclude Chapter Two, the ship of my narrative sails forward, guided by the steady light of purpose. The North Star remains a constant in the ever-changing seas, a principle that not only directs the journey but infuses it with meaning and significance. In the next chapters, the narrative will continue, exploring the winds of change, the storms of adversity, and the uncharted territories where the North Star beckons.

As we sail through the waters of Chapter Two, it becomes apparent that the search for a North Star is not just about reaching a point on the horizon; it's about the journey itself. The act of defining success, identifying personal goals, and crafting a vision becomes a transformative voyage, shaping not only the destination but the very essence of the sailor.

As I stand on the precipice of the open sea, ready to cast off and embrace the transformative voyage that lies ahead, I extend an invitation to you. An invitation to cast off with me, to set sail into the unknown, and to embrace the journey of a thousand waves with courage, resilience, and an unwavering belief in the treasures that await beyond the horizon.

Discovering one's North Star is not always a straightforward endeavor. It may involve exploring different paths, experimenting with various options, and overcoming obstacles along the way. Furthermore, it is important to recognize that the North Star may evolve and change as individuals grow, learn, and transform throughout their lives. However, the rewards of finding one's North Star are significant, as it can provide a sense of clarity, direction, and fulfillment, guiding individuals towards a purposeful and meaningful existence.

.

CHAPTER 3

WEATHERING THE STORM

"In the midst of winter, I found there was, within me, an invincible summer."

- Albert Camus

Weathering the Storm of life like a sailor at sea is a chapter that explores how to cope with the challenges and uncertainties that life throws at us. It draws inspiration from the experiences of sailors who have faced fierce storms at sea and learned to sail in high winds.

The song "Weathering the Storm" by Ryan Stevenson featuring Gabby Barrett resonated deeply with me, as it beautifully captures the essence of finding hope and faith in God during difficult times. The lyrics convey a powerful message:

"When the clouds roll in
And the sky grows dark
And I don't know where You are
I will lift my hands
And trust Your heart
You're the light that guides me through
You're the calm inside the chaos
You're the peace inside the pain
You're the strength when I am weak
You're the anchor in the waves
You're the God who stays
The same through every season
You're the reason I can say
I'm weathering the storm."

These lyrics not only inspire, but they also engrave within

me the attributes of the millionaire's offshore mindset.

Just as the song speaks of finding light, calm, peace, and strength amidst the challenges, the mindset of millionaires offshore embraces resilience, unwavering determination, and a trust in the larger forces at play. It reminds me that even in the face of uncertainty and adversity, there is a steadfastness and an anchor that guides us through the storms. This mindset is essential in weathering the challenges that come our way and finding the courage and strength to persevere.

As our journey continues, the sea of life inevitably presents storms – tempests that test the resilience and mettle of every sailor. Chapter Three is a testament to the strength found in weathering these storms, revealing the invaluable lessons learned in the face of adversity.

Section A: Resilience and Perseverance

Life is not always smooth sailing. Storms will come, testing our resolve and challenging our determination. In this chapter, we delve into the power of resilience and perseverance, discovering how these traits can help us weather the storms that inevitably arise on our journey to success.

1. Overcoming Setbacks

Setbacks are an inevitable part of life, but it is how we respond to them that defines our path forward. We will explore stories of individuals who faced significant setbacks

In times of crisis, there are often hidden opportunities waiting to be discovered. In this section, we will explore how successful individuals have been able to identify and capitalize on these opportunities, turning adversity into advantage.

Resilience is the anchor that prevents us from drifting into despair when faced with life's tempests. Through gripping narratives and personal accounts, we explore the stories of individuals who, like seasoned sailors, weathered the storms with unwavering resilience. This section unveils the power of the human spirit to endure, adapt, and emerge stronger from the trials encountered on the open sea.

Section B: Strategies for Staying Afloat in Difficult Times

Surviving storms is not merely about enduring; it's about navigating through them. In this section, we delve into practical strategies employed by those who successfully sailed through turbulent times. From maintaining a steady course to finding refuge in the eye of the storm, readers are equipped with a toolkit of insights to navigate their own challenges. The chapter emphasizes that storms are not detours but integral parts of the journey, shaping sailors into capable navigators.

1. Navigating Economic Downturns

Economic downturns can be turbulent and challenging, but they also present unique opportunities for those who are prepared. We will examine case studies of individuals and businesses that not only weathered economic storms but also thrived during these periods of uncertainty. By studying their strategies and approaches, we can learn valuable lessons on how to navigate and capitalize on economic downturns.

2. Innovating in the Face of Change

Change is a constant force that shapes the world around us. In times of crisis, innovation becomes a powerful tool for adaptation and growth. We will explore stories of individuals who have embraced change and used it as a catalyst for innovation and success. By understanding their creative approaches and mindset, we can learn how to foster innovation in our own lives and businesses.

Section C: Cultivating a Growth Mindset

A growth mindset is essential for weathering the storms of life and emerging stronger on the other side. In this section, we will delve into the principles and practices that allow individuals to cultivate a growth mindset, enabling them to navigate challenges with resilience and determination.

1. Embracing a Positive Mindset

A positive mindset is a cornerstone of resilience. We will explore techniques and practices that help individuals develop and maintain a positive outlook, even in the face of adversity. By adopting a positive mindset, we can overcome obstacles, stay motivated, and attract opportunities that align with our goals and aspirations.

2. Building Emotional Resilience

As we navigate through Chapter Three, the message becomes clear: storms are not to be feared but faced. Each trial, like a wave crashing against the hull, refines the sailor, teaching lessons that calm seas seldom can. It is within the tumultuous moments that resilience is forged, and the true strength of character emerges.

Emotional resilience is the ability to adapt and bounce back from difficult situations. We will explore strategies for building emotional resilience, including self-care, stress management, and developing healthy coping mechanisms. By cultivating emotional resilience, we can maintain our well-being and effectively navigate the storms that come our way.

As we journey through this chapter, we will discover the power of resilience, perseverance, and a growth mindset in navigating the storms of life. We will learn from those who have overcome setbacks and adversity, spotting opportunities in times of crisis and embracing change as a catalyst for growth. By adopting these lessons, we can weather any storm and emerge stronger, ready to continue our journey towards success.

So, dear reader, brace yourself for the tempests ahead, for in weathering the storms, you not only survive but learn to dance with the waves, mastering the art of sailing through life's unpredictable currents.

CHAPTER 4

UNCHARTED WATERS

"There are no shortcuts to any place worth going."
- Beverly Sills

The "Uncharted Waters" video game series holds a special

place in my heart as one of my favorites. Produced by Koei under its "Rekoeition" brand, this Japanese simulation and role-playing series immerses players in the thrilling world of sailing, trading, and adventure during the Age of Discovery. It beautifully captures the spirit of exploration and the challenges faced by captains and commodores as they navigate the vast seas.

Within the series, players assume the roles of ambitious characters driven by their dreams and aspirations. In the first title, "Uncharted Waters," released in 1990, players embody Leon Franco, a young Portuguese noble who seeks to restore his family's glory. They engage with nations such as Portugal, Spain, and the Ottoman Empire, investing in ports, discovering new lands, and undertaking tasks for the King of Portugal.

"Uncharted Waters: New Horizons," released in 1994, expands the series further. Players can choose from six different characters, each with their own unique stories, goals, and nationalities. This installment introduces eight nations, including Portugal, Spain, England, France, the Netherlands, Italy, Turkey, and Morocco. It allows players to explore the world, engage in commerce, combat, and diplomacy, and encounter both historical and fictional events.

The latest addition to the series, "Uncharted Waters Origin," released in 2023, serves as a remarkable remake of the first two games, featuring improved graphics, sound, and gameplay. It offers players an enhanced experience with eight national powers, 200 ports, 60 villages, over 300 battlegrounds, and a dynamic weather system comprising over 20 types of weather. Additionally, the game introduces a multiplayer mode, enabling players to cooperate or compete with one another, fostering a sense of community and shared adventures.

The allure of the "Uncharted Waters" series lies not only in its captivating gameplay and immersive world but also in its ability to evoke the spirit of exploration and the pursuit of dreams. It resonates with the theme of our book, as both explore the uncharted territories of life—whether through virtual seas or real-life endeavors. Just as the characters in the game face challenges, overcome obstacles, and discover new horizons, our book encourages readers to embrace the unknown, cultivate resilience, and embark on their own journeys of self-discovery and growth.

Uncharted waters are a metaphor for the unknown and uncertain situations that we face in life. They can be challenging, risky, or even frightening, but they can also offer opportunities for learning, growth, and discovery. Some examples of uncharted waters in life are:

- Starting a new career or business
- Moving to a new place or country
- Facing a health crisis or a personal loss
- Pursuing a passion or a dream
- Making a major decision or a change

In essence, "Uncharted Waters" serves as a testament to the human spirit's indomitable desire for exploration and adventure, inviting us to chart our own paths, seize opportunities, and navigate the uncharted waters of life with courage and determination.

Section A: Embracing the Unknown

Life is full of surprises and unexpected turns. In this chapter, we dive into the realm of uncharted waters, exploring the courage and adaptability required to navigate unfamiliar territory. By embracing the unknown, we can unlock new possibilities and chart a course towards unimagined success.

1. Stepping Outside the Comfort Zone

The comfort zone is a place of familiarity and security, but it can also be a barrier to growth and exploration. We will explore the importance of stepping outside our comfort zones and embracing new experiences. By pushing our boundaries, we can discover hidden strengths and talents that will propel us forward in uncharted waters.

2. Embracing Change and Uncertainty

Change and uncertainty are constants in life, and our ability to embrace them is crucial for success. We will delve into techniques for cultivating a mindset that embraces change, allowing us to adapt and thrive in uncertain environments. By relinquishing our fear and resistance to the unknown, we open ourselves up to infinite possibilities.

Section B: Innovative Thinking and Problem-Solving

In uncharted waters, traditional solutions may not apply. In this section, we explore the importance of innovative thinking and problem-solving skills in navigating unfamiliar territory. By cultivating our creativity and resourcefulness, we can overcome obstacles and forge new paths to success.

1. Cultivating a Culture of Innovation

Innovation is the lifeblood of progress. We will examine

strategies for fostering a culture of innovation, both in our personal lives and within organizations. By encouraging creativity, collaboration, and a willingness to take risks, we can unlock new ideas and approaches that will guide us through uncharted waters.

2. Adaptive Problem-Solving

Uncharted waters often present unique challenges that require adaptive problem-solving skills. We will explore methods for thinking critically, analyzing complex situations, and finding creative solutions. By honing our problem-solving abilities, we can navigate uncharted waters with confidence and resilience.

Section C: Embracing Failure and Learning

Failure is an inevitable part of any journey, particularly when venturing into uncharted waters. In this section, we will explore the importance of embracing failure as a valuable learning experience. By reframing our perspective and leveraging failure as a stepping stone to success, we can grow stronger and wiser in the face of uncertainty.

1. Embracing a Growth Mindset

A growth mindset is crucial for navigating uncharted waters. We will delve into the principles of a growth mindset, which includes embracing challenges, persisting in the face of setbacks, and seeing failure as an opportunity to learn and improve. By adopting a growth mindset, we can approach new and unfamiliar situations with confidence and resilience.

2. Extracting Lessons from Failure

Failure is not the end but a stepping stone to success. We will explore techniques for extracting valuable lessons from failure, including reflection, self-evaluation, and feedback analysis. By learning from our mistakes and adjusting our approach, we can refine our strategies and increase our chances of success in uncharted waters.

To navigate uncharted waters, we need to have courage, curiosity, and creativity. We also need to have a sense of direction, a plan, and a backup plan. We need to be flexible, adaptable, and resilient. We need to seek help and support from others when we need it. And we need to enjoy the journey, not just the destination.

As we sail through the uncharted waters of life, this chapter reminds us of the importance of embracing the unknown, fostering innovative thinking, and learning from failure. By stepping outside our comfort zones, adapting to change, and cultivating a growth mindset, we can navigate uncharted waters with confidence and chart a path towards extraordinary achievements. So, set sail and embrace the thrill of the unknown, for it is in uncharted waters that our greatest discoveries await.

CHAPTER 5

ANCHORS AWEIGH

"Anchor Aweigh, my boys, Anchor Aweigh!"

- Charles A. Zimmerman

Anchors Aweigh is a phrase that means to raise the anchors of a ship and prepare to sail. It is also the title of a song that is the official march of the United States Naval Academy and the unofficial anthem of the United States Navy. The song was composed in 1906 by Charles A. Zimmermann, a lieutenant and the bandmaster of the Naval Academy, with lyrics by Alfred Hart Miles, a midshipman. The song expresses the pride and spirit of the Navy and its sailors.

Anchors Aweigh is also the name of a 1945 musical comedy film starring Frank Sinatra, Kathryn Grayson, and Gene Kelly. The film tells the story of two sailors on a four-day leave in Hollywood, who meet a young boy and his aunt, an aspiring singer, and try to help her get an audition with José Iturbi, a famous conductor and pianist. The film features several songs and dances, including a famous scene where Kelly dances with Jerry Mouse, the cartoon character from Tom and Jerry.

As we navigate the seas of opportunity, Chapter Five unfurls its sails, guiding us through the intricate dance of wealth-building strategies. Anchors Aweigh becomes the anthem, urging sailors to hoist their financial sails high and set course for the prosperity that awaits on the horizon.

As we embark on the journey of wealth-building strategies, Chapter Five hoists its sails and guides us through the intricate dance of financial success. Just as "Anchors Aweigh" signifies the raising of ship anchors and setting sail, it becomes our anthem, urging us to elevate our financial aspirations and chart a course towards the prosperity that lies on the horizon.

1. Unleashing the Spirit of Financial Freedom:

"Anchors Aweigh" is not only a phrase, but it also encompasses the essence of liberation and progress. We explore the concept of financial freedom, where we release the anchors that hold us back and embrace the possibilities of wealth creation. It is a call to set sail on a path of abundance and independence.

2. Navigating the Seas of Opportunity:

Like skilled sailors, we learn to navigate the vast seas of opportunity that lie before us. We delve into various wealth-building strategies, understanding the power of investments, entrepreneurship, and smart financial planning. By honing our skills and knowledge, we steer our financial ships towards prosperity.

3. Cultivating a Wealth Mindset:

Anchors Aweigh reminds us of the importance of cultivating a wealth mindset. We explore the psychology of abundance, embracing positivity, and shifting our perspectives towards opportunities rather than limitations. By adopting a mindset that attracts wealth, we set ourselves up for success on our financial voyage.

4. Hoisting the Sails of Financial Literacy:

Just as sails catch the wind and propel a ship forward, we recognize the significance of financial literacy. We delve into the world of personal finance, learning about budgeting, investing, and managing debt. Equipped with this knowledge, we secure a strong foundation for our financial journey.

Section A: Investments and Financial Planning
Determining Your Core Values

In this chapter, we explore the importance of establishing strong anchors in our lives—our core values. These values serve as guiding principles that keep us grounded and help us make decisions aligned with our true selves. By understanding and embracing our core values, we can navigate the complexities of life with clarity and purpose.

1. Reflecting on Personal Values

Our values shape our beliefs, attitudes, and actions. We will embark on a journey of self-reflection to identify and define our personal values. By understanding what truly matters to us, we can establish a solid foundation from which to make choices and navigate the challenges and opportunities that arise.

2. Aligning Actions with Values

Identifying our core values is just the first step; living in alignment with them is equally important. We will explore strategies for aligning our actions with our values, ensuring that our daily choices reflect what we hold dear. By living authentically and in harmony with our values, we can cultivate a sense of fulfillment and lead a purpose-driven life.

The journey to financial success is akin to a well-planned voyage. In this section, we explore the art of investments and financial planning, unraveling the secrets of individuals who strategically deployed their resources. From building robust investment portfolios to understanding risk and return, readers gain insights into the financial strategies that set the course for long-term prosperity.

Section B: Harnessing Offshore Opportunities for Prosperity

Cultivating Meaningful Relationships

Meaningful connections with others are essential for our well-being and success. In this section, we delve into the importance of cultivating healthy and supportive relationships that enrich our lives and provide a sense of belonging.

1. Nurturing Authentic Connections

Authenticity is the cornerstone of meaningful relationships. We will explore strategies for building and nurturing authentic connections, such as active listening, empathy, and vulnerability. By fostering genuine relationships, we create a support network that anchors us in times of uncertainty and provides a sense of belonging.

2. Surrounding Yourself with Positive Influences

The company we keep has a significant impact on our mindset and actions. We will discuss the importance of surrounding ourselves with positive influences—people who inspire and uplift us. By intentionally seeking out individuals who align with our values and aspirations, we can create a circle of support that encourages our growth and success.

Just as a seasoned sailor leverages favorable winds, successful individuals often explore offshore opportunities to amplify their wealth. This section serves as a guide to navigating the international waters of finance. From understanding tax implications to tapping into global markets, readers embark on a journey that expands their financial horizons and explores the untapped potential of offshore ventures.

As we traverse through Anchors Aweigh, it becomes apparent that financial success is not a solitary island but a chain of strategic decisions and well-calculated risks. The chapter emphasizes that, like a ship casting off its anchor, individuals must free themselves from financial constraints and set sail towards the boundless sea of prosperity.

Section C: Creating Balance and Self-Care
To navigate the seas of life effectively, we must prioritize self-care and create a sense of balance. In this section, we focus on nurturing our well-being and establishing healthy routines that replenish our energy and maintain our resilience.

1. Prioritizing Self-Care
Self-care is not a luxury; it is a necessity. We will explore various self-care practices, including physical, mental, and

emotional well-being. By prioritizing self-care, we replenish our energy, reduce stress, and cultivate a strong foundation from which to face life's challenges.

2. Establishing Work-Life Balance

Achieving a healthy work-life balance is crucial for our overall well-being. We will discuss strategies for setting boundaries, managing time effectively, and integrating activities that bring us joy and fulfillment. By creating harmony between our personal and professional lives, we can prevent burnout and maintain a sustainable pace in our pursuits.

As we navigate the seas of life, this chapter reminds us of the importance of anchoring ourselves in our core values, cultivating meaningful relationships, and prioritizing self-care. By staying true to our values, surrounding ourselves with positive influences, and nurturing our well-being, we can confidently set sail towards a fulfilling and purposeful life. So, anchors aweigh, and let the winds of purpose carry us towards our dreams and aspirations.

Conclusion:

As we conclude Chapter Five's exploration of wealth-building strategies, we embrace the spirit of "Anchors Aweigh." With determination and foresight, we set sail towards prosperity, guided by the anthem of financial freedom. By unleashing our potential, navigating opportunities, cultivating a wealth mindset, and hoisting the sails of financial literacy, we embark on a transformative journey. Together, let us navigate the seas of opportunity, propelled by the winds of financial success, towards a future abundant with prosperity and fulfillment.

So may the winds of financial wisdom fill your sails, and may you navigate the waters of wealth with confidence and foresight. Anchors Aweigh—a call to embark on a journey where financial mastery becomes the wind that propels you toward the shores of enduring prosperity.

CHAPTER 6

45

GLOBAL HORIZONS

"The best education I have ever received was through travel."
- Lisa Ling

I am from Lagos State in Nigeria, widely recognized as the center of excellence and renowned for its breathtaking aquatic splendor, my roots trace back to the illustrious Dosumu family. While I take pride in my noble heritage, I yearned to venture beyond the familiar shores and seek my own fortunes. In this chapter, we embark on a journey that transcends local boundaries, and together, we explore the transformation from a local perspective to global horizons.

In the expansive canvas of Chapter Six, we set our sights on the vast horizon of international success stories. The chapter unfolds as a world map, revealing the profiles of individuals who found prosperity abroad and showcasing the transformative power of embracing global perspectives for personal growth.

1. Embracing the Spirit of Exploration:

Despite the rich heritage of the Dosumu family, I harbored a deep desire to explore uncharted territories and carve out my own path. We delve into the motivations and aspirations that propel individuals to venture beyond the confines of their local environment. Embracing the spirit of exploration, we unlock the doors to endless possibilities.

2. Navigating the Global Landscape:

As I ventured offshore, I found myself navigating the vast expanse of the global landscape. We delve into the challenges and triumphs of immersing oneself in diverse cultures, markets, and opportunities. We explore the skills and perspectives needed to adapt and thrive in the global arena, transcending geographical limitations.

3. Unleashing the Power of Networking:

In this chapter, we recognize the power of building connections and networks that span beyond local boundaries. We delve into strategies for establishing meaningful relationships, fostering collaboration, and leveraging the strength of a global network to open doors to new opportunities and enhance personal growth.

4. Embracing Cultural Diversity:

Global horizons bring forth a tapestry of cultures, traditions, and perspectives. We explore the richness of diversity and the importance of embracing cultural differences. By cultivating cultural intelligence, we gain a competitive edge and foster meaningful connections in a globalized world.

The Paradise Papers

Have you read the Paradise Papers? I suggest you do. It chronicles a list of persons who found their fortunes in millions offshore! Some of them have become billionaires today. But that is a subject of discuss for another day. Now we only keep our eyes on the millionaires in global horizons.

The Paradise Papers is a collection of leaked financial documents that surfaced in 2017, offering insight into offshore investments and potential tax evasion by individuals and companies worldwide. The leak, comprising 13.4 million documents, was acquired by the German newspaper Süddeutsche Zeitung and shared with the International Consortium of Investigative Journalists (ICIJ).

Originating from Appleby, a Bermuda-based law firm, as well as other offshore service providers, these documents shed light on the financial activities of various entities. Among those implicated were multinational corporations, wealthy individuals, politicians, and public figures.

The Paradise Papers exposed the complex web of offshore financial practices, often involving tax havens, intricate corporate structures, and offshore accounts. While such practices can be legal, they can also be employed for illicit purposes, including tax evasion, money laundering, and asset concealment.

The leaked documents unveiled instances where individuals and companies exploited legal loopholes and offshore jurisdictions to minimize their tax obligations or shield their wealth from scrutiny. The involvement of major multinational corporations, celebrities, politicians, and public officials in offshore financial activities was also brought to attention.

For example:

Jackie Chan: The martial arts star and actor was among the celebrities named in the Panama Papers. He had at least six companies managed through the law firm Mossack Fonseca, although he has not been accused of any wrongdoing.

Lewis Hamilton: The Formula One champion was revealed in the Paradise Papers to have avoided paying taxes on his private jet by using a complex scheme involving an Isle of Man company.

Shakira: The Colombian singer was also named in the Paradise Papers. She reportedly transferred the rights to her songs to a company in Malta, where the corporate tax rate is much lower than in Spain, where she lives.

Andrew Mason: He is the founder and former CEO of Groupon, a popular online platform for deals and discounts. He became a millionaire when Groupon went public in 2011, but he was fired in 2013 after the company's stock price plummeted. He then moved to Berlin, where he launched a new venture called Descript, a podcast editing software.

Mathew Mullenwag: He is the co-founder and CEO of Automattic, the company behind WordPress, the most widely used blogging platform in the world. He is also a lead developer of the open source WordPress software. He has a net worth of over $400 million, and he runs his company from various locations around the world, such as San Francisco, New York, and Houston.

These are just some of the world famous millionaires who found their fortunes offshore.
The release of the Paradise Papers sparked global attention and ignited debates regarding the ethics and legality of offshore tax planning. Consequently, tax authorities in numerous countries initiated investigations and inquiries,

resulting in legal actions and policy reforms aimed at enhancing transparency and combating tax evasion.

It is crucial to note that not all individuals and entities mentioned in the Paradise Papers engaged in illegal activities. Offshore financial structures can serve legitimate purposes, such as facilitating international business transactions and safeguarding assets. Nonetheless, the leak highlighted the potential for abuse and misuse of these structures, raising concerns about fairness, accountability, and the integrity of the global financial system.

While the examples we provided are indeed notable individuals, it's important to recognize that the Paradise Papers implicated a wide range of people and entities, and their inclusion in the leak does not necessarily imply wrongdoing. The papers served as a catalyst for global scrutiny of offshore financial activities and prompted discussions on how to address the challenges associated with offshore tax practices

Section A: Embracing Globalization

In an interconnected world, understanding and embracing globalization is essential. In this chapter, we explore the significance of expanding our horizons and engaging with diverse cultures, ideas, and perspectives. By embracing global awareness, we can broaden our understanding of the world and make a positive impact on a global scale.

1. Recognizing the Power of Diversity

Diversity is a strength that fuels innovation and progress. We will explore the importance of embracing cultural, ethnic, and ideological diversity. By valuing and respecting different perspectives, we can foster an inclusive global community that celebrates the richness of human experiences.

2. Developing Cultural Competence

Cultural competence is the ability to interact effectively with people from different cultures. We will delve into the skills and attitudes necessary to develop cultural competence, such as empathy, open-mindedness, and adaptability. By understanding and appreciating cultural nuances, we can build meaningful connections and navigate cross-cultural interactions with sensitivity and respect.

Embarking on a journey beyond borders, we delve into the lives of those who sought success in foreign lands. Through captivating narratives, we discover the challenges faced and triumphs achieved by individuals who ventured across cultural and geographical boundaries. These stories serve as beacons, illuminating the possibilities that arise when one embraces the richness of diversity and taps into the global tapestry of opportunities.

Section B: Global Citizenship

Being a global citizen means recognizing our interconnectedness and taking responsibility for the well-being of the world. In this section, we explore the concept of global citizenship and the role each of us can play in creating positive change.

1. Understanding Global Issues

Global challenges, such as climate change, poverty, and inequality, require collective action. We will delve into pressing global issues and their interconnected nature. By staying informed and engaged, we can contribute to solutions and advocate for a more sustainable and equitable world.

2. Taking Action Locally and Globally

Global citizenship starts with local action. We will discuss ways in which individuals can make a difference, both in their immediate communities and on a global scale. By volunteering, supporting causes, and engaging in advocacy, we can amplify our impact and promote positive change worldwide.

Beyond financial gains, international experiences offer invaluable lessons that shape personal growth. This section explores the impact of diverse cultures, cross-cultural collaborations, and global perspectives on an individual's journey. From broadening worldviews to fostering adaptability, readers gain insights into how embracing the global horizon becomes a catalyst for profound personal development.

Back home in Nigeria we have remarkable individuals who have found millions offshore. Tunde Ednut, Mark Angel, Linda Ikeji, and Victor Osimeh are some of the most successful and famous Nigerians in their respective fields. Here is a brief summary of who they are and what they do:

- Tunde Ednut: He is a blogger, comedian, entertainer and musician who is known for his controversial and viral posts on Instagram. He has over 2 million followers on his former Instagram account, which was deactivated in 2020. He created a new account in 2021 and gained over 1 million followers in less than a week. He is also a singer who has released songs like "Jingle Bell" and "Catching Cold". He is estimated to be worth ₦890 million.

- Mark Angel: He is a comedian, scriptwriter, and video producer who is the founder of Mark Angel Comedy, a YouTube channel that features funny skits and pranks. He is best known for his collaboration with Emmanuella Samuel, a child comedian who is his niece. He has over 7 million subscribers on YouTube and has won several awards, such as the African Digital Awards and The Future Awards Africa. He is estimated to be worth ₦1.2 billion.

- Linda Ikeji: She is a blogger, writer, entrepreneur and media personality who is the founder of Linda Ikeji's Blog, one of the most visited blogs in Nigeria. She covers topics such as entertainment, celebrity news, politics, and lifestyle. She also owns Linda Ikeji TV, an online streaming platform that produces original content. She is one of the richest and most influential bloggers in Africa. She is estimated to be worth ₦6 billion .

- Victor Osimeh: He is a professional footballer who plays as a striker for Napoli in the Italian Serie A and the Nigeria national team. He started his career at Ultimate Strikers Academy in Lagos before moving to Europe. He has played for clubs such as Wolfsburg, Charleroi, and Lille. He is regarded as one of the most promising and talented young players in the world. He is estimated to be worth ₦3.4 billion

These are just some of the notable Nigerians who have distinguished themselves and are millionaires. There are many other successful Nigerian entrepreneurs who have made their mark in various fields and industries. Here are some of them:

- Cosmas Maduka: He is the founder and CEO of Coscharis Group, a conglomerate that deals in automobiles, agriculture, ICT, logistics, and more. He started his business with only ₦200 and grew it into a multi-billion naira empire. He is also the sole distributor of BMW cars in Nigeria.

- Jason Njoku: He is the co-founder and CEO of iROKOtv, the largest online platform for African movies and TV shows. He is also a partner at Spark, a venture capital firm that invests in Nigerian startups. He is one of the leading figures in the Nigerian tech ecosystem and has been featured in Forbes, CNN, and BBC.

- Tara Fela-Durotoye: She is the founder and CEO of House of Tara, a leading beauty and cosmetics brand in Nigeria. She is also a pioneer of the bridal makeup profession and a mentor to thousands of young women. She is a recipient of several awards and recognitions, such as the Africa Awards for Entrepreneurship and the Young Global Leader by the World Economic Forum.

These are just some of the other successful Nigerian entrepreneurs who have achieved remarkable feats and inspired many others.

As we sail through Chapter Six, it becomes evident that success is not confined by borders but flourishes in the expanses of a connected world. The international stage becomes a platform for individuals to showcase their talents, learn from different cultures, and create a tapestry of experiences that enriches their personal narrative.

Section C: Cultural Exchange and Collaboration

Cultural exchange and collaboration are catalysts for mutual understanding and innovation. In this section, we explore the benefits of cross-cultural collaboration and the transformative power of sharing ideas and experiences.

1. Fostering International Partnerships

International partnerships foster collaboration, innovation, and mutual growth. We will discuss the importance of seeking opportunities for collaboration across borders, whether in business, academia, or the arts. By embracing diverse perspectives and working together, we can create solutions that transcend geographical boundaries.

2. Exploring Travel and Study Abroad

Travel and study abroad experiences offer invaluable opportunities for personal and professional growth. We will explore the benefits of immersing ourselves in different cultures, languages, and environments. By stepping outside our comfort zones and embracing new experiences, we gain a broader perspective and develop a global mindset.

As we embark on a journey towards global horizons, this chapter reminds us of the importance of embracing globalization, cultivating global citizenship, and fostering cultural exchange. By valuing diversity, taking action to address global challenges, and engaging in cross-cultural collaboration, we can contribute to a more interconnected and harmonious world. So, let us set sail towards global horizons, united in our commitment to creating a brighter future for all.

Conclusion:

As Chapter 6 draws to a close, we reflect on the transformative journey from Lagos to global horizons. While anchored in the proud Dosumu family heritage and the splendor of Lagos State, we have ventured offshore to seek our own fortunes and expand our horizons. By embracing the spirit of exploration, navigating the global landscape, unleashing the power of networking, and embracing cultural diversity, we have embarked on a remarkable voyage of personal and professional growth.

Together, we celebrate the boundless opportunities that await beyond local boundaries. Let us embrace the challenges and triumphs of the global arena, guided by the lessons learned and insights gained. As we navigate the intricacies of a world without borders, we emerge as individuals who have transcended local limitations, poised to make a difference in an interconnected and diverse world.

May the stories of global horizons inspire you to set sail beyond the familiar, to embrace the opportunities that lie in the unexplored territories of our interconnected world. In Chapter Six, the world becomes your oyster, inviting you to discover the pearls of success woven into the fabric of diverse cultures and global collaborations.

CHAPTER 7

SAILING THROUGH ECONOMIC STORMS

"The fishermen know that the sea is dangerous and the storm terrible, but they have never found these dangers sufficient reason for remaining ashore."
- Vincent Van Gogh

In the unpredictable seas of the global economy, Chapter Seven unfurls as a guide to navigating through economic storms. This chapter, akin to a sturdy ship, provides insights into strategies for adapting to market changes, weathering financial turbulence, and emerging stronger on the other side.

Economic storms of life are periods of financial hardship or instability that can affect individuals, businesses, or nations. They can be caused by various factors, such as recessions, inflation, unemployment, debt, trade wars, natural disasters, pandemics, or political turmoil. Economic storms of life can have negative impacts on people's income, savings, investments, consumption, and well-being. They can also create opportunities for innovation, adaptation, and resilience.

Some examples of economic storms of life are:
- The Great Depression of the 1930s, which was the longest and deepest economic downturn in modern history, affecting millions of people around the world. It was triggered by the stock market crash of 1929 and worsened by the Dust Bowl, a severe drought that devastated the US agricultural sector.

- The Global Financial Crisis of 2007-2009, which was the most severe financial crisis since the Great Depression, affecting the banking system, the housing market, and the global economy. It was caused by the collapse of the subprime mortgage market and the failure of several major financial institutions.

- The COVID-19 Pandemic of 2020-2021, which was the worst public health crisis in a century, affecting millions of lives and livelihoods around the world. It caused unprecedented disruptions to economic activity, trade, travel, and social interactions, leading to a sharp contraction of the global economy and a rise in poverty and inequality.

There are different ways to cope with economic storms of life, depending on the situation and the resources available. Some general strategies are:

- Building a solid financial foundation, such as having an emergency fund, paying off debts, saving for retirement, and investing wisely.

- Diversifying income sources, such as having multiple streams of income, developing new skills, or starting a side hustle.

- Staying adaptable and flexible, such as being open to new opportunities, learning from mistakes, and embracing change.

- Seeking professional guidance, such as consulting a financial planner, an accountant, or a lawyer, depending on the needs and goals.

Section A: Understanding Economic Turbulence

Economic storms are inevitable in the ever-changing landscape of global markets. In this chapter, we explore the strategies and mindset required to navigate through economic downturns and emerge stronger on the other side. By understanding the nature of economic turbulence and preparing ourselves, we can weather the storms with resilience and adaptability.

1. Recognizing the Cycles of the Economy
Economic cycles consist of periods of expansion and contraction. We will delve into the characteristics of these cycles and examine the factors that contribute to economic downturns. By understanding the patterns and causes of economic turbulence, we can better prepare ourselves for the challenges that lie ahead.

2. Assessing the Impact on Individuals and Businesses
Economic storms affect individuals and businesses differently. We will explore the potential impacts of economic downturns on employment, investments, and financial stability. By assessing the potential consequences, we can develop strategies to mitigate risks and seize opportunities for growth.

Like the ever-shifting tides, markets are dynamic and subject to constant change. This section explores the art of adapting to market fluctuations, sharing stories of individuals who not only survived economic storms but thrived by understanding and leveraging market dynamics. From technological shifts to evolving consumer preferences, readers gain insights into staying agile and resilient in the face of change.

Section B: Building Financial Resilience

Building financial resilience is essential for sailing through economic storms. In this section, we delve into strategies for managing personal and business finances effectively, ensuring stability and preparedness in the face of economic uncertainty.

1. Establishing Emergency Funds

Emergency funds provide a financial safety net during times of instability. We will discuss the importance of establishing and maintaining emergency funds, which can help cover unexpected expenses and provide peace of mind during economic downturns.

2. Diversifying Income Streams and Investments

Relying on a single income stream or investment can leave us vulnerable during economic storms. We will explore the benefits of diversifying income sources and investments, spreading risk and increasing the likelihood of financial stability. By diversifying our financial portfolio, we can navigate economic turbulence with greater confidence.

Lessons from Economic Downturns

Economic downturns, much like storms at sea, can be formidable challenges. This section delves into the lessons learned from navigating through economic downturns. Through real-world examples and pragmatic advice, readers discover how individuals turned adversity into opportunity during challenging economic climates. The chapter emphasizes that economic storms, while daunting, can be transformative, leading to innovations, efficiencies, and renewed perspectives.

As we traverse Chapter Seven, the message is clear: economic storms are inevitable, but the skills acquired in navigating through them become invaluable. The ability to adapt, innovate, and persevere becomes the compass that guides sailors through turbulent financial waters.

Section C: Adapting and Innovating in Challenging Times

Adaptability and innovation are key to thriving in turbulent economic conditions. In this section, we explore strategies for adapting our mindset, business models, and approaches to seize opportunities and overcome challenges.

1. Embracing a Growth Mindset

A growth mindset is crucial for navigating economic storms. We will discuss the importance of embracing challenges, persevering in the face of setbacks, and viewing failures as opportunities for learning and growth. By cultivating a growth mindset, we can adapt to changing circumstances and find creative solutions to economic challenges.

2. Innovating and Seeking Opportunities

Economic storms often create new opportunities for innovation and growth. We will explore strategies for identifying emerging trends, adapting business models, and seizing opportunities in challenging times. By staying agile and open to change, we can position ourselves and our businesses for success, even amidst economic uncertainty.

As we sail through the unpredictable waters of economic storms, this chapter reminds us of the importance of understanding economic turbulence, building financial resilience, and embracing adaptability and innovation. By preparing ourselves, diversifying our financial strategies, and staying agile, we can navigate economic storms with resilience and emerge stronger on the other side. So, let us set sail with confidence, knowing that we have the tools and mindset to overcome economic challenges and chart a course towards prosperity.

Survive the economic tempest and thrive amidst uncertainty. Take hold of the helm, embrace the challenges, and chart your course to triumph. Now is the time to set sail, armed with knowledge and determination. Equip yourself with the tools, strategies, and resilience to conquer economic storms. Embrace the winds of change and seize the opportunities that await. In the unpredictable seas of the global economy, may you emerge not only unscathed but strengthened by the challenges faced, ready to navigate the next wave of opportunities that await on the horizon. The journey begins now.

CHAPTER 8

CHARTING THE GLOBAL LANDSCAPE

"The pessimist complains about the wind; the optimist expects it to change; the realist adjusts the sails."
- William Arthur Ward

The shifting tides of our global landscape encompass a wide array of transformations, spanning politics, economics, society, and the environment. Several key factors contribute to these dynamic changes:

1. The ebb and flow of great powers, including the United States, China, Russia, and the European Union, shapes the global stage as they navigate competition and collaboration across diverse realms such as trade, security, human rights, and climate change.

2. The emergence and impact of groundbreaking technologies like artificial intelligence, biotechnology, nanotechnology, and quantum computing have far-reaching implications for innovation, productivity, governance, and ethical considerations.

3. Globalization presents both challenges and opportunities, as our world becomes increasingly interconnected and interdependent. The risks and rewards of global integration and fragmentation influence diverse aspects of our lives, from economic systems to cultural exchange and the exchange of ideas.

4. Climate change poses profound effects on our planet, triggering more frequent and intense natural disasters,

biodiversity loss, ecosystem degradation, population migration, and displacement. Governments, businesses, and civil society entities respond with mitigation and adaptation strategies.

These examples highlight only a fraction of the multifaceted elements within the ever-evolving dynamics of our global landscape.

Now, it is crucial to recognize and engage with these changes. By understanding the complexities and interconnections at play, we can actively shape the future. Let us embrace the challenges and opportunities presented by this shifting terrain, collaborating across borders and disciplines to forge a prosperous and sustainable world for generations to come.

As our voyage continues, Chapter Eight unfolds as a detailed map, guiding individuals through the complexities of the global landscape. This chapter explores the opportunities and challenges of venturing into international waters, providing insights into the strategies for success amidst diverse cultures and markets.

Section A: The Changing Dynamics of the Global Landscape

The global landscape is constantly evolving, shaped by geopolitical shifts, technological advancements, and societal changes. In this chapter, we explore the importance of understanding and navigating the complexities of the global landscape. By charting the global landscape, we can adapt to emerging trends, identify opportunities, and make informed decisions in an interconnected world.

1. Geopolitical Dynamics and Power Shifts
Geopolitical dynamics play a significant role in shaping the global landscape. We will examine the evolving power dynamics among nations, regional alliances, and geopolitical hotspots. By understanding these dynamics, we can anticipate potential impacts on various aspects such as international trade, security, and diplomacy.

2. Technological Advancements and Digital Transformation
Technological advancements are transforming the global landscape at an unprecedented pace. We will explore emerging technologies, such as artificial intelligence, blockchain, and renewable energy, and their impact on various industries and societies. By embracing technology and understanding its implications, we can adapt to the digital age and leverage its potential for innovation and growth.

Exploring Cross-Border Opportunities

The world is a vast sea of opportunities, and in this section, we set sail to explore the potential beyond one's own shores. Through case studies and real-life examples, readers discover the intricacies of venturing into cross-border opportunities. From understanding cultural nuances to navigating legal complexities, individuals learn the art of expanding their horizons and tapping into the wealth of possibilities beyond borders.

Section B: Navigating Global Opportunities and Risks

The global landscape presents a multitude of opportunities and risks. In this section, we delve into strategies for identifying and navigating these opportunities and risks, enabling us to make informed decisions in a rapidly changing world.

1. Identifying Emerging Markets and Industries

Emerging markets and industries offer new frontiers for growth and innovation. We will discuss strategies for identifying and capitalizing on emerging opportunities, such as understanding market trends, conducting market research, and forming strategic partnerships. By staying informed and adaptable, we can navigate the global landscape and seize emerging opportunities.

2. Managing Global Risks and Uncertainties

Global risks, such as economic downturns, climate change, and cybersecurity threats, require effective risk management strategies. We will explore approaches to assess and mitigate risks, such as diversifying supply chains, implementing robust cybersecurity measures, and adopting sustainable practices. By proactively managing risks, we can safeguard our interests and navigate uncertainties in the global landscape.

International Networking for Success

In the interconnected seas of global business, networking becomes a powerful compass for success. This section explores the importance of international networking, providing practical tips on building meaningful connections across continents. From leveraging technology to attending global events, readers gain insights into creating a robust network that transcends geographical boundaries.

As we journey through Chapter Eight, it becomes evident that the global landscape is not just a vast expanse but a canvas of opportunities waiting to be explored. Charting this landscape requires a combination of cultural intelligence, strategic thinking, and a willingness to embrace diversity.

Section C: Embracing Intercultural Competence

Intercultural competence is crucial for operating in a globalized world. In this section, we focus on the importance of embracing diversity, fostering cross-cultural understanding, and cultivating effective communication skills in global interactions.

1. Cross-Cultural Communication and Collaboration

Cross-cultural communication is essential for building trust, resolving conflicts, and fostering collaboration in diverse settings. We will explore effective communication strategies, such as active listening, cultural sensitivity, and adaptability. By embracing cross-cultural competence, we can bridge cultural gaps and build meaningful connections in a globalized world.

2. Embracing Diversity and Inclusion

Diversity and inclusion are catalysts for innovation and success in the global landscape. We will discuss the importance of embracing diversity, creating inclusive environments, and leveraging diverse perspectives. By fostering a culture of diversity and inclusion, we can tap into the collective wisdom and creativity of people from different backgrounds, driving progress in the global landscape.

As we navigate the global landscape, this chapter reminds us of the importance of understanding geopolitical dynamics, embracing technological advancements, and cultivating intercultural competence. By charting the global landscape, identifying opportunities and risks, and embracing diversity, we can thrive in an interconnected world and contribute to positive global change. So, let us set our course, armed with knowledge and a global perspective, as we navigate the ever-evolving global landscape with confidence and purpose.

Dear reader, may the insights from Chapter Eight empower you to navigate the global landscape with confidence. As you set sail into international waters, may you find success by not only understanding the seas you navigate but by appreciating the unique beauty and challenges each region brings to your journey.

CHAPTER 9

THE HIDDEN COMPASS

"Your passion is the hidden compass that points you towards your destiny."

- Steve Jobs

The concept of the hidden compass refers to an internal guiding force or intuition that helps individuals navigate through life's challenges and decisions. It represents a deep sense of knowing and direction that may not always be apparent or easily explained. The hidden compass serves as a metaphorical tool that can guide individuals towards their true purpose, values, and authentic selves.

In the intricate dance of life, Chapter Nine reveals the significance of intuition and decision-making, serving as a hidden compass that guides sailors through the uncharted waters of choices and opportunities.

Section A: Section A: Uncovering Our Inner Compass
Within each of us lies a hidden compass—a guiding force that helps us navigate life's challenges and make meaningful decisions. In this chapter, we delve into the concept of the hidden compass and explore how we can tap into our inner wisdom to find direction and purpose.

1. Connecting with Our Authentic Selves
To uncover our hidden compass, we must first connect with our authentic selves. We will explore the importance of self-

reflection, introspection, and self-awareness in understanding our values, passions, and aspirations. By embracing our true selves, we can align our choices and actions with our core principles.

2. Cultivating Intuition and Inner Wisdom

Intuition is a powerful tool that can guide us in uncertain times. We will discuss the significance of cultivating intuition and accessing our inner wisdom. By developing mindfulness practices, listening to our inner voice, and trusting our instincts, we can tap into our hidden compass and make decisions aligned with our deepest desires.

Trusting Your Instincts

Much like a sailor relying on the subtle cues of the wind and waves, this section explores the importance of trusting one's instincts. Through personal stories and anecdotes, readers discover the power of intuition in decision-making. Whether in business ventures or personal choices, the hidden compass within becomes a reliable guide in navigating through uncertainty.

The hidden compass is often associated with intuition, inner wisdom, or gut feelings. It is believed to go beyond logical reasoning and taps into a deeper level of understanding and insight. While it may not always align with external expectations or societal norms, the hidden compass is considered a reliable source of guidance for personal growth and decision-making.

Trusting the hidden compass requires individuals to cultivate self-awareness, listen to their inner voice, and pay attention to their emotions and instincts. It involves tuning into one's values, desires, and passions to make choices that align with their authentic selves.

The hidden compass can be particularly useful in times of uncertainty or when faced with complex decisions. It provides a sense of clarity and purpose, helping individuals navigate through challenges, overcome obstacles, and find their way forward.

However, it's important to note that the hidden compass is not infallible. It should be balanced with critical thinking, rational analysis, and consideration of practical factors. While intuition and the hidden compass can offer valuable insights, they should be complemented by a thoughtful evaluation of facts and potential consequences.

Section B: Navigating Life's Crossroads
Life is filled with crossroads—moments when we must make important choices that shape our paths. In this section, we

explore strategies for navigating these crossroads with clarity and confidence, guided by our hidden compass.

1. Clarifying Our Values and Priorities

Our values and priorities serve as guiding principles when facing life's crossroads. We will discuss the importance of clarifying our values and aligning our choices with what truly matters to us. By staying true to our core principles, we can make decisions that bring us closer to a fulfilling and purpose-driven life.

2. Embracing Change and Embracing Uncertainty

Crossroads often involve change and uncertainty. We will explore strategies for embracing change and navigating uncertainty with resilience and adaptability. By reframing challenges as opportunities for growth, embracing a growth mindset, and cultivating flexibility, we can navigate life's crossroads with courage and grace.

Making Sound Choices in the Business World

Decision-making in the business world requires a unique set of skills. This section delves into the strategies employed by successful individuals when faced with crucial choices. From risk assessment to strategic planning, readers gain insights into the art of making sound decisions that align with their goals. The chapter emphasizes the importance of balancing intuition with informed choices to steer a course towards success.

As we sail through life, it becomes evident that the hidden compass is not a mystical force but a culmination of experiences, knowledge, and self-awareness. Trusting this compass becomes a skill honed through the journey, enabling individuals to navigate the unpredictable currents of life with a steady hand on the helm.

Section C: Living a Purpose-Driven Life
Our hidden compass guides us toward a purpose-driven life—a life filled with meaning and fulfillment. In this section, we delve into strategies for aligning our actions with our purpose, allowing us to make a positive impact and find deep satisfaction in our endeavors.

1. Discovering Our Life's Purpose
Discovering our life's purpose is a transformative journey. We will explore exercises and practices for uncovering our passions, values, and unique contributions to the world. By aligning our actions with our purpose, we can create a life that is filled with meaning and fulfillment.

2. Taking Inspired Action
Living a purpose-driven life requires taking inspired action.

We will discuss strategies for setting meaningful goals, overcoming obstacles, and staying motivated on our path. By taking intentional steps aligned with our purpose, we can make a lasting impact and leave a positive legacy.

Hidden Compass is also the name of an exceptional online publication that captivates readers with its remarkable narratives, showcasing the frontiers of human exploration and knowledge. Through compelling storytelling, they delve into a diverse range of subjects such as travel, science, culture, art, and history. This platform embraces and celebrates the passions of individuals, recognizing that everyone possesses their own unique areas of expertise.

Their latest issue, The 2023 Pathfinder Issue, centers around the inspiring journey of Tété-Michel Kpomassie, the first African to explore Greenland. The expedition was inspired by a book that Tété encountered in the 1950s, which painted vivid descriptions of a distant frozen land. This ignited an eight-year odyssey from his equatorial home to the Arctic, becoming a monumental achievement in African exploration.

Decades later, Lola Akinmade Åkerström, a storyteller of Nigerian descent, discovered Tété's book, "An African in Greenland," and found herself deeply connected to his story. She yearned to follow in his footsteps and journey to

Greenland.

The 2023 Pathfinder Prize presented itself as an extraordinary opportunity for Åkerström. Gathering her team, which included fellow Nigerian-born writer and photographer Noo Saro-Wiwa and Swedish videographer Erik Jaråker, they embarked on a cultural expedition to Greenland in April 2023, seeking to unravel the question of who has the right to tell a place's story.

Welcome to In Tété's Footsteps: The 2023 Pathfinder Issue of Hidden Compass—a remarkable collection of stories dedicated entirely to the expedition. This issue invites readers to immerse themselves in the experiences, discoveries, and encounters of this remarkable journey.

Ultimately, embracing the hidden compass means acknowledging and honoring one's inner guidance system. By trusting and following this internal compass, individuals can embark on a personal journey that leads them towards a more fulfilling and authentic life path. In the exploration of our inner selves, this chapter serves as a poignant reminder of the significance in connecting with our authentic essence.

It highlights the value of nurturing our intuition and confidently maneuvering through the crossroads of life. By embracing a purpose-driven existence, guided by our innate wisdom, we can forge a life that is truly meaningful and gratifying. Let us embark upon this journey of self-discovery, placing our trust in the hidden compass within us, as it directs us towards a path illuminated by purpose, joy, and fulfillment.

May your personal voyage lead you to the unveiling of your own hidden compass. Amidst the vast array of choices that lay before you, may this chapter be a steadfast companion, reminding you that the answers often reside within, eagerly waiting to be discovered and embraced. As you navigate the unpredictable waters of life, may you find confidence in the decisions you make and may your hidden compass be a reliable guide, steering you towards a future brimming with possibility and authenticity.

CHAPTER 10

SAILING AGAINST THE

WIND

"Smooth seas do not make skillful sailors."
- Franklin D. Roosevelt

In the vast expanse of life's ocean, Chapter Ten invites sailors to navigate against the wind, breaking through barriers and conquering challenges that stand in the way of their journey. This chapter unfolds as an anthem to resilience and determination, showcasing stories of individuals who dared to sail against the prevailing winds.

Sailing against the wind, also known as beating or tacking, is a sailing technique that involves navigating a boat in a direction opposite to the wind's natural course. It requires skill, strategy, and careful maneuvering to make progress against the prevailing wind.

When sailing against the wind, a sailboat cannot simply travel directly into it due to the physics of sail propulsion. Instead, sailors must utilize a technique called tacking. Tacking involves sailing at an angle to the wind, known as a close-hauled or close reach position, and then changing direction periodically to zigzag towards the desired destination. This maneuver allows the boat to take advantage of the wind's force and make progress against it.

Sailing against the wind presents a unique set of challenges. The wind's resistance can slow down the boat's speed and make navigation more difficult. It requires constant adjustments and coordination between the crew and the helmsperson to maintain balance and control.

However, there are situations where sailing against the wind becomes necessary. It may be the only option when trying to reach a destination directly upwind or when circumnavigating an obstruction. Skilled sailors often embrace the challenge, considering it an opportunity to showcase their sailing abilities and problem-solving skills.

Metaphorically, sailing against the wind can represent overcoming obstacles and facing adversity in life. It symbolizes perseverance, determination, and the ability to navigate through challenging circumstances. Just as sailors adjust their course and tactics to make progress against the wind, individuals who sail against the wind in life must adapt, be resilient, and find alternative paths to achieve their goals.

Sailing against the wind teaches valuable lessons about resilience, patience, and the importance of staying focused on the destination despite the challenges encountered along the way. It reminds us that even when faced with adversity, it is possible to make headway and reach our intended destination with determination, skill, and perseverance.

Section A: Embracing Challenges and Resistance
Life often presents us with challenges that seem insurmountable, obstacles that seem impossible to overcome. In this chapter, we explore the concept of sailing against the wind—the ability to persevere, adapt, and thrive in the face of adversity.

1. Embracing the Growth Mindset
A growth mindset is essential when sailing against the wind. We will delve into the importance of cultivating resilience, embracing challenges as opportunities for growth, and reframing setbacks as stepping stones to success. By adopting a growth mindset, we can transform obstacles into catalysts for personal and professional development.

2. Building Emotional Resilience
Emotional resilience is the foundation for navigating challenges. We will discuss strategies for managing stress, developing emotional intelligence, and cultivating a positive mindset. By building emotional resilience, we can face adversity with grace, maintain perspective, and stay motivated in the face of obstacles.

Overcoming Societal Challenges

Society's currents can be powerful, but this section explores the stories of individuals who faced and overcame societal challenges. From cultural norms to biases, readers discover how these sailors navigated against societal winds to carve their unique paths. The chapter encourages individuals to challenge norms, embrace authenticity, and chart courses that reflect their true selves.

Section B: Section B: Strategies for Overcoming Resistance

Overcoming resistance requires strategic thinking and perseverance. In this section, we explore strategies for navigating through resistance and forging our own path, even when faced with opposition.

1. Developing a Clear Vision and Purpose

A clear vision and a strong sense of purpose provide the fuel needed to sail against the wind. We will explore techniques for clarifying our vision, setting meaningful goals, and staying focused during challenging times. By anchoring ourselves in our purpose, we can navigate the stormy seas and stay on course.

2. Cultivating Adaptability and Flexibility

Adaptability and flexibility are vital when sailing against the wind. We will discuss the importance of embracing change, being open to new possibilities, and adjusting our strategies when necessary. By remaining agile and adaptable, we can navigate unexpected obstacles and find alternative routes to success.

Pioneering Paths to Success

Success often requires forging new trails, and this section celebrates the pioneers who sailed against the wind to achieve greatness. Through case studies and narratives, readers gain insights into the strategies employed by those who ventured into unexplored territories, paving the way for others to follow. This chapter becomes a guide for those ready to break free from the conventional and set sail towards uncharted success.

As we navigate through Chapter Ten, the message resounds: sailing against the wind is not a hindrance but an opportunity. The challenges faced become the very winds that propel sailors forward, creating a momentum that propels them toward new horizons.

Section C: Persevering with Determination

Perseverance is the key to sailing against the wind. In this section, we explore strategies for staying determined and resilient, even when the odds seem stacked against us.

1. Building a Support Network

A strong support network can provide invaluable encouragement and guidance along the journey. We will discuss the importance of surrounding ourselves with positive and like-minded individuals who can offer support, advice, and inspiration. By fostering relationships with supportive people, we can draw strength from their presence and persevere in the face of adversity.

2. Learning from Setbacks and Failures

Setbacks and failures are inevitable when sailing against the wind. We will explore strategies for learning from these experiences, embracing them as opportunities for growth, and leveraging the lessons learned to propel us forward. By viewing setbacks as stepping stones, we can turn adversity into fuel for success.

As we sail against the wind, this chapter reminds us of the importance of embracing challenges, building emotional resilience, and persevering with determination. By adopting a growth mindset, developing strategies for overcoming resistance, and staying true to our vision and purpose, we can navigate the stormy waters of life with resilience and strength. So, let us set sail with unwavering determination, knowing that we have the power to overcome any obstacle and achieve greatness, even when faced with the strongest winds.

Dear reader, may this chapter inspire you to unfurl your sails and navigate against the prevailing winds. In the face of challenges, may you find the strength to persevere, embracing the winds of adversity as the very forces that will carry you towards your unique and extraordinary destination.

CHAPTER 11

THE WEALTHY ARCHIPELAGO

"Tax havens are the dark side of globalization."
Jeffrey Sachs

Amidst the vast sea of opportunities, Chapter Eleven unveils the importance of diversifying investments and building a resilient financial archipelago. This chapter serves as a guide to creating a network of wealth, navigating through the intricacies of investments and maintaining a balance between risk and reward.

Section A: Redefining Wealth

The concept of the wealthy archipelago is a metaphor that compares the different aspects of wealth and well-being to a group of islands. Each island represents a dimension of wealth, such as financial, physical, mental, social, spiritual, or environmental. The islands are interconnected by bridges, which symbolize the relationships and interactions between the different dimensions. The goal of the wealthy archipelago is to achieve a balance and harmony among the islands, so that each one contributes to the overall well-being of the individual and the community.

The concept of the wealthy archipelago was developed by Dr. Riza Mantaring, a Filipino financial expert and author of the book The Wealthy Archipelago: A Holistic Approach to Wealth. In her book, she explains how to apply the concept to personal finance, investing, and life planning. She also provides practical tips and tools to help readers assess their current situation, identify their goals, and create a roadmap to achieve them. She argues that wealth is not just about money, but about living a meaningful and fulfilling life.

The concept of the wealthy archipelago is based on the idea that wealth is multidimensional and subjective. It recognizes that different people have different definitions and preferences of wealth, depending on their values, beliefs, and aspirations. It also acknowledges that wealth is dynamic and evolving, as it changes over time and across different contexts. Therefore, the concept of the wealthy archipelago encourages people to be flexible, adaptable, and resilient in pursuing their wealth and well-being.

Wealth is often associated with financial abundance, but in this chapter, we explore the concept of the wealthy archipelago—a holistic approach to wealth that encompasses various dimensions of well-being. By redefining wealth, we can cultivate a more balanced and fulfilling life.

1. Beyond Financial Wealth

Financial wealth is just one aspect of a rich and fulfilling life. We will delve into other dimensions of wealth, such as physical health, mental and emotional well-being, relationships, personal growth, and contribution to society. By expanding our definition of wealth, we can strive for a more comprehensive and meaningful experience.

2. The Pursuit of Well-being

Well-being is the foundation of a wealthy archipelago. We will explore strategies for nurturing physical health through exercise, nutrition, and self-care. Additionally, we will discuss practices for enhancing mental and emotional well-being, fostering positive relationships, and pursuing personal growth. By prioritizing well-being, we can create a solid base for a fulfilling and abundant life.

Strategies for Building a Robust Portfolio

Like a skilled navigator plotting a course through various islands, this section explores the art of building a diversified investment portfolio. Readers discover the strategies employed by successful individuals to create a resilient financial foundation. From stocks and bonds to real estate and alternative investments, this chapter serves as a compass for constructing a well-rounded portfolio that can weather various economic tides.

Section B: Cultivating Abundance Mindset

An abundance mindset is essential for embracing the wealthy archipelago. In this section, we explore techniques for shifting our mindset and cultivating a belief in the abundance that surrounds us.

An abundance mindset is a psychological and philosophical perspective that focuses on the belief that there are ample resources, opportunities, and possibilities available in the world. It is the opposite of a scarcity mindset, which is characterized by the belief that resources are limited and that one must compete for a share of those resources.

Individuals with an abundance mindset approach life with a sense of optimism, gratitude, and possibility. They believe that there is enough for everyone and that success, happiness, and fulfillment are not finite resources. They tend to view setbacks and challenges as temporary and see them as opportunities for growth and learning.

Some key characteristics and beliefs associated with an abundance mindset include:

1. Gratitude: Individuals with an abundance mindset appreciate and focus on what they have rather than dwelling on what they lack. They recognize the abundance in their lives and express gratitude for it.

2. Collaboration: People with an abundance mindset believe in collaboration and cooperation rather than competition. They understand that by working together, they can create more opportunities and achieve greater success for themselves and others.

3. Growth mindset: They embrace a growth mindset, which means they believe that their abilities and intelligence can be developed through effort, learning, and perseverance. This mindset enables them to see challenges as opportunities for growth and improvement.

4. Positive outlook: Those with an abundance mindset tend to have a positive outlook on life. They focus on possibilities, solutions, and opportunities rather than dwelling on problems or limitations.

5. Generosity: An abundance mindset often leads to a willingness to share resources, knowledge, and opportunities with others. They believe in the principle of giving and

understand that by helping others, they can contribute to the overall abundance of the world.

Cultivating an abundance mindset can have a profound impact on various aspects of life, including relationships, career, and personal well-being. It can lead to increased confidence, resilience, and creativity, as well as improved problem-solving skills and the ability to embrace change.

It is important to note that developing an abundance mindset is a mindset shift that takes time and practice. It involves challenging and reframing limiting beliefs and adopting a more positive and expansive perspective. By consciously focusing on abundance and cultivating gratitude, individuals can gradually shift their mindset and experience the benefits of an abundance mentality.

1. Embracing Gratitude and Appreciation
Gratitude and appreciation are powerful practices that shift our focus from scarcity to abundance. We will discuss techniques for cultivating a daily gratitude practice, acknowledging the blessings in our lives, and appreciating the abundance that exists within and around us. By fostering an attitude of gratitude, we can attract more abundance and fulfillment.

2. Letting Go of Scarcity Mentality

Scarcity mentality can hinder our ability to embrace the wealthy archipelago. We will explore strategies for identifying and releasing limiting beliefs around scarcity, scarcity mindset, and lack. By reframing our thoughts and beliefs, we can create a mindset of abundance and tap into the wealth of opportunities available to us.

Balancing Risk and Reward

Every island in the financial archipelago comes with its own set of risks and rewards. This section delves into the delicate balance between risk and reward in investment decisions. Through case studies and practical advice, readers gain insights into managing risks while maximizing potential returns. The chapter emphasizes the importance of calculated decisions and a long-term vision in building a wealthy archipelago.

Section C: Aligning Wealth with Purpose

Aligning our wealth with purpose brings a deeper sense of fulfillment and meaning. In this section, we explore the importance of connecting our wealth with our values and passions.

1. Defining Personal Values

Personal values serve as a compass for aligning wealth with

purpose. We will discuss approaches to identify and define our core values, exploring what truly matters to us. By aligning our financial decisions and actions with our values, we can create a sense of coherence and integrity in our lives.

2. Impactful Wealth and Contribution
Wealth presents an opportunity for making a positive impact in the world. We will explore ways to leverage our resources, skills, and influence to contribute to society and create meaningful change. By aligning our wealth with purposeful contribution, we can experience a profound sense of fulfillment and leave a lasting legacy.

As we embrace the concept of the wealthy archipelago, this chapter reminds us of the importance of redefining wealth, cultivating an abundance mindset, and aligning our wealth with purpose. By nurturing our well-being, embracing gratitude and abundance, and infusing our wealth with values and contribution, we can create a truly wealthy and fulfilling life. So, let us embark on the journey to the wealthy archipelago, exploring the vast dimensions of wealth and discovering the abundance that lies within us and around us.

As we sail through Chapter Eleven, the metaphor of the archipelago becomes a symbol of financial resilience and stability. Just as diverse islands create a robust ecosystem, a well-diversified investment portfolio becomes a stronghold against market volatility.

Dear reader, may this chapter guide you in building your own wealthy archipelago, where each investment is a sturdy island contributing to the strength and stability of your financial journey. May you navigate through the seas of wealth with wisdom, ensuring that your financial archipelago stands strong against the currents of change.

CHAPTER 12

LEGACY OF THE CAPTAIN

"The captain of a ship can run a great ship, but he can't do anything about the tides."
-Michael Bloomberg

The legacy of a captain refers to the lasting impact and influence that a captain leaves behind through their leadership, actions, and achievements. Captains, whether in the context of sports teams, military units, or other leadership roles, often have a significant impact on their teams and organizations, shaping their culture, performance, and future success.

As our journey progresses, Chapter Twelve invites sailors to reflect on the legacy they are crafting — a legacy that transcends personal success and extends to making a lasting impact on the world. This chapter explores the importance of creating a legacy and giving back, becoming a beacon for future generations.

Section A: Section A: Defining a Lasting Legacy

In this chapter, we explore the concept of the legacy of the captain—the imprint we leave behind on the world and the lasting impact we have on future generations. We reflect on what it means to create a meaningful legacy and how we can strive to leave a positive mark on the world.

1. The Power of Purpose and Values

A lasting legacy is built upon a strong foundation of purpose and values. We will delve into the significance of clarifying our personal purpose and defining our core values. By aligning our actions with our purpose and living in accordance with our values, we can shape a legacy that reflects our authentic selves.

2. Ripple Effects and the Butterfly Effect

Every action we take has the potential to create ripple effects and influence the lives of others. We will explore the butterfly effect—the idea that small actions can lead to significant consequences. By understanding the interconnectedness of our choices and their impact on the world, we can make conscious decisions that contribute to a positive and far-reaching legacy.

Creating a Lasting Impact

Beyond accumulating wealth, individuals often aspire to leave a lasting impact on the world. This section explores the stories of those who have gone beyond personal success to contribute meaningfully to society. Through philanthropy, mentorship, and community engagement, readers discover how individuals have shaped their legacies by making a positive impact on the lives of others.

One of the most profound legacies I am aware of is encapsulated in the saying, "the captain goes down with the ship." This maritime tradition emphasizes the captain's responsibility for the well-being of their vessel and crew, signifying that they should be the last to leave or perish onboard. Beyond its literal meaning, this expression serves as a powerful metaphor representing principles of loyalty, duty, and sacrifice. It highlights the captain's unwavering commitment to their duties and their willingness to put the needs of their crew and the vessel above their own safety. This legacy resonates with the values of leadership, selflessness, and honor, reminding us of the profound impact that individuals can have when they prioritize the welfare and collective good above personal considerations.

Another aspect of a captain's legacy is their ability to inspire and motivate those under their command. A great captain possesses strong leadership skills, communication abilities, and a clear vision that inspires their team members to work together towards a common goal. They lead by example, demonstrating integrity, resilience, and dedication, which can instill these qualities in their team members and leave a lasting impression on their character.

Another important aspect of a captain's legacy is their ability to foster a positive and supportive team culture. A captain who creates an environment of trust, respect, and collaboration can enhance team cohesion, morale, and performance. Their legacy may include a reputation for building strong relationships, resolving conflicts, and creating a sense of unity within the team.

Section B: Living with Integrity and Authenticity
Living with integrity and authenticity is key to leaving a legacy that resonates with others. In this section, we delve into the importance of staying true to ourselves and embodying our values in every aspect of our lives.

1. Authentic Leadership
Authentic leadership is about leading with integrity, transparency, and vulnerability. We will discuss the qualities of an authentic leader and explore strategies for cultivating authenticity in our own lives. By embracing our unique strengths and vulnerabilities, we can inspire others and leave a lasting impact through our genuine presence.

2. Leading by Example

Our actions speak louder than words when it comes to leaving a legacy. We will explore the power of leading by example and how our behaviors and choices influence those around us. By embodying the values and principles we wish to see in the world, we can inspire others to follow suit and create a positive ripple effect.

Balancing Success with Social Responsibility

Success, when coupled with social responsibility, becomes a powerful force for positive change. This section delves into the concept of balancing success with giving back. Whether through sustainable business practices or charitable endeavors, readers gain insights into how successful individuals have integrated social responsibility into their journeys. The chapter becomes a guide for those seeking not only financial prosperity but also a legacy of compassion and contribution.

Captains also leave a legacy through their achievements and the results they achieve with their teams. Their ability to strategize, make critical decisions under pressure, and execute plans effectively can lead to success in competitions or achieving organizational objectives. These accomplishments become a part of the captain's legacy, showcasing their skill, determination, and ability to lead their team to victory.

Furthermore, a captain's legacy may extend beyond their immediate team or organization. Their influence and impact can inspire future generations of leaders and serve as a benchmark for excellence. The lessons learned from their leadership style, values, and approach to challenges can resonate with others and shape the way leadership is practiced in the future.

As we navigate through Chapter Twelve, the importance of steering toward a legacy becomes clear. The captain's legacy is not just about personal accomplishments but about the ripples of positive influence that extend far beyond the individual.

Section C: Empowering Others and Paying It Forward

A significant part of creating a lasting legacy involves empowering others and paying it forward. In this section, we discuss the importance of investing in the growth and development of others and how it contributes to a legacy of positive change.

1. Mentorship and Guidance

Mentorship and guidance play a crucial role in empowering others. We will explore the benefits of mentorship and strategies for providing support, guidance, and encouragement to those who come after us. By sharing our knowledge, experiences, and wisdom, we can help others navigate their own journeys and make a meaningful impact.

2. Creating Systems of Change

To leave a legacy that transcends our individual efforts, we must create systems of change. We will discuss the significance of identifying systemic issues, advocating for justice and equality, and working towards creating a more equitable and sustainable world. By addressing root causes and working collectively, we can create lasting change that impacts future generations.

The Legacy of the Captain can be understood in various contexts, each with its own significance. These contexts include:

1. The Legacy of Captain Sir Tom Moore:

Captain Sir Tom Moore, a British war veteran and fundraiser, left an enduring legacy through his remarkable achievements. His determination to support NHS charities during the Covid-19 pandemic by walking laps in his garden before turning 100 captured the nation's hearts. He became a symbol of hope and resilience, raising over £38 million. His recognition included a knighthood, honors, and tributes.

Sadly, he passed away in February 2021 from Covid-19. His family established the Captain Tom Foundation, which continues his charitable work, particularly in areas such as mental health, education, and combating loneliness.

2. The Legacy of Captain America:

Captain America, a beloved fictional superhero and leader of the Avengers in the Marvel Cinematic Universe, has his own distinctive legacy. Created through the Super-Soldier serum, he fought against Nazis and Hydra during World War II. After being frozen in ice for 70 years, he returned to protect the world with the Avengers. Captain America's iconic vibranium shield symbolized his courage and honor. In an alternate timeline, he retired and passed on his mantle and shield to Sam Wilson, also known as the Falcon, ensuring his legacy lives on.

3. The Legacy of Captain James Cook:

Captain James Cook, a British explorer and navigator, made significant contributions during his three voyages across the Pacific Ocean in the 18th century. He meticulously mapped the coastlines of Australia, New Zealand, Hawaii, and other islands, while also establishing contact with indigenous peoples. Cook's observations and documentation of astronomical phenomena, such as the transit of Venus and solar eclipses, were groundbreaking. However, his legacy is complex, as he is both celebrated as one of history's greatest explorers and criticized for the lasting impact his encounters had on cultures and environments. His life came to a tragic end in 1779 when he was killed by Hawaiian natives following a dispute over a stolen boat.

In summary, the Legacy of the Captain encompasses the enduring impact left by notable individuals such as Captain Sir Tom Moore, Captain America, and Captain James Cook. Their contributions range from inspiring acts of charity and heroism to exploration and discovery, shaping the lives of countless people and leaving a lasting imprint on history.

Ultimately, the legacy of a captain is measured by the lasting impact they have on individuals, teams, and organizations. It is reflected in the memories, stories, and lessons shared by those who have been influenced by their leadership. A captain's legacy is a testament to their leadership abilities, character, and the positive change they brought about during their time in charge.

As we reflect on the legacy of the captain, this chapter reminds us of the importance of defining our purpose and values, living with integrity and authenticity, and empowering others. By embracing our unique leadership qualities, leading by example, and investing in the growth and development of others, we can create a legacy that inspires and uplifts. So, let us embark on this journey of creating a meaningful and lasting legacy, knowing that our actions today have the power to shape a better tomorrow for generations to come.

May this chapter inspire you to contemplate the legacy you are shaping. May you set sail with a compass that points not only towards personal success but also towards a legacy of impact and contribution. In the grand tapestry of life, may your legacy be a testament to the enduring power of a life well-lived.

CHAPTER 13

RAISING THE SAILS OF INNOVATION

"The biggest risk is not taking any risk. In a world that is changing quickly, the only strategy that is guaranteed to fail is not taking risks."

- Mark Zuckerberg

"Raising the sails of innovation" is a metaphorical expression that refers to the act of initiating or propelling innovative ideas, projects, or initiatives. It captures the essence of setting in motion the process of creativity and progress.

In the context of innovation, "raising the sails" represents the initial step of harnessing the power and potential of new ideas. It signifies the moment when individuals or organizations make a deliberate effort to embrace change, seek out novel solutions, and explore uncharted territories.

In the ever-evolving sea of opportunities, Chapter Thirteen

unfurls as an exploration of the role of innovation in the journey towards success. This chapter sets sail with the stories of entrepreneurs as innovators, showcasing how groundbreaking ideas and forward-thinking propel individuals beyond the horizon of conventional achievements.

Section A: Unleashing the Power of Innovation

In this chapter, we explore the transformative force of innovation and how it propels us forward into new frontiers. We delve into the mindset, strategies, and practices that enable us to raise the sails of innovation and navigate uncharted waters.

1. Embracing a Culture of Innovation

A culture of innovation is the fertile ground in which new ideas flourish. We discuss the importance of fostering a culture that encourages creativity, experimentation, and risk-taking. By creating an environment that values innovation, we can inspire and empower individuals to think outside the box and generate groundbreaking solutions.

2. Embracing Change and Adaptability

Innovation requires a willingness to embrace change and adapt to evolving circumstances. We explore strategies for cultivating a mindset that is open to new ideas, flexible in the face of uncertainty, and resilient in times of adversity. By embracing change, we can harness its potential and turn it into opportunities for growth and innovation.

Entrepreneurs as Innovators

Much like skilled sailors adapting to changing winds, entrepreneurs navigate the seas of innovation. This section delves into the experiences of those who have harnessed creativity to disrupt industries and pioneer new paths. Through real-world examples, readers explore the mindset and strategies that transform entrepreneurs into innovators, shaping the landscape of their industries.

Just as raising the sails on a ship captures the wind's energy and propels the vessel forward, raising the sails of innovation involves tapping into the collective imagination, knowledge, and resources to drive positive change. It involves creating an environment that encourages creativity, fosters a growth mindset, and promotes the exploration of new possibilities.

Raising the sails of innovation requires several key elements:

1. Vision: A clear vision or goal that inspires and motivates individuals or organizations to embark on an innovative journey.

2. Open-mindedness: A willingness to challenge conventional thinking, embrace new perspectives, and consider unconventional approaches.

3. Creativity: Encouraging and nurturing creativity and imagination within individuals or teams, fostering an environment that supports idea generation and experimentation.

4. Collaboration: Recognizing that innovation often thrives through collaboration and diverse perspectives, and fostering an environment that encourages teamwork, knowledge-sharing, and interdisciplinary collaboration.

5. Risk-taking: Embracing calculated risks and accepting that not all innovative endeavors may succeed, while understanding that failure can be a valuable learning opportunity.

6. Continuous Learning: Cultivating a culture of continuous learning and improvement, where individuals and organizations are open to feedback, adapt to changing circumstances, and iterate on ideas and approaches.

Section B: Nurturing the Seeds of Innovation

In this section, we uncover the essential elements that nurture and foster innovation. We delve into the practices and approaches that ignite creativity, spark curiosity, and encourage breakthrough thinking.

1. Curiosity and Continuous Learning

Curiosity does not kill the cat rather it is the fuel that drives innovation. We discuss the importance of cultivating a curious mindset and embracing a lifelong commitment to learning. By expanding our knowledge, exploring diverse perspectives, and seeking out new experiences, we can fuel our creative thinking and unlock innovative solutions.

2. Collaboration and Diversity

Innovation thrives in collaborative and diverse environments. We explore the power of collaboration, the benefits of diverse teams, and the strength of inclusive decision-making. By embracing different perspectives, harnessing collective intelligence, and fostering an inclusive culture, we can generate innovative ideas that transcend individual limitations.

Adapting to Technological Advancements

In the modern era, technological advancements are the winds that drive innovation. This section explores how individuals have embraced and adapted to the rapid changes in technology, leveraging them to propel their ventures forward. From embracing digital transformation to incorporating cutting-edge solutions, readers gain insights into how staying at the forefront of technological progress becomes a catalyst for success.

"Raising the Sails of Innovation" is a noteworthy PhD thesis authored in 2022 by Lucien von Schomberg, a philosopher who delves into the concept and complexities of Responsible Innovation (RI). This approach aims to guide innovation processes towards outcomes that are socially desirable and ethically acceptable, particularly in addressing the pressing "grand challenges" of our time, such as climate change and food security.

The thesis comprehensively examines the historical, political, and conceptual aspects of Responsible Innovation. It argues that the prevailing economic notion of innovation often hampers the achievement of the societal ideal of Responsible Innovation. Von Schomberg highlights the need to redefine and broaden the understanding of innovation to encompass its societal dimensions and impact.

Furthermore, the thesis proposes a novel political concept of Responsible Innovation that emphasizes the importance of co-creation and democratic participation by all stakeholders in society. It advocates for an inclusive approach that involves active engagement from various actors, including researchers, policymakers, industry representatives, civil society organizations, and citizens. By involving diverse perspectives and encouraging democratic deliberation, this new concept of Responsible Innovation aims to ensure that innovation aligns with societal values and addresses the needs and concerns of different stakeholders.

In essence, "Raising the Sails of Innovation" presents a thought-provoking exploration of Responsible Innovation, shedding light on the challenges and opportunities associated with steering innovation towards more socially and ethically responsible outcomes. The thesis contributes to the ongoing discourse on the role of innovation in addressing complex societal issues and offers a compelling vision for a more inclusive, participatory, and responsible approach to shaping our technological future.

As we sail through Chapter Thirteen, it becomes evident that innovation is not a distant island but a dynamic force that propels individuals towards new horizons. The ability to raise the sails of innovation is a skill that transforms challenges into opportunities, ensuring that entrepreneurs remain at the forefront of their respective fields.

Section C: Overcoming Barriers to Innovation

Innovation is not without its challenges. In this section, we address common barriers to innovation and explore strategies for overcoming them.

1. Fear of Failure and Risk Aversion

Fear of failure and risk aversion can stifle innovation. We discuss techniques for reframing failure as a learning opportunity, embracing calculated risks, and creating a safe environment for experimentation. By shifting our mindset around failure and risk, we can create the space for innovation to thrive.

2. Breaking Free from the Status Quo

Breaking free from the status quo is essential for driving innovation forward. We delve into strategies for challenging conventional thinking, questioning assumptions, and fostering a culture of constructive dissent. By encouraging critical thinking and pushing boundaries, we can overcome complacency and pave the way for transformative innovation.

As we raise the sails of innovation, this chapter reminds us of the power of embracing a culture of innovation, nurturing curiosity and collaboration, and overcoming barriers to innovation. By fostering an environment that encourages creativity, embracing change, and nurturing the seeds of innovation, we can embark on a journey of continuous discovery and drive positive change in our lives, organizations, and society as a whole. So, let us set sail with the winds of innovation, propelled by our boundless curiosity and the belief that we have the power to shape a better future through our innovative ideas and actions.

Raising the sails of innovation is about embracing the unknown, challenging the status quo, and actively seeking out opportunities for improvement and growth. It is a dynamic and ongoing process that requires perseverance, resilience, and a commitment to fostering a culture that embraces innovation at all levels. By doing so, individuals and organizations can chart new courses, discover new horizons, and create positive change in their respective fields.

CHAPTER 14

CALM WATERS AND SUNSET DREAMS

"Sunsets are proof that no matter what happens, every day can end beautifully."
- Kristen Butler

Calm waters and sunset dreams evoke a sense of tranquility, beauty, and introspection. These natural scenes have captivated poets, artists, and dreamers throughout history, inspiring a multitude of interpretations and emotions.

As our journey reaches a contemplative juncture, Chapter Fourteen invites sailors to set their course toward the tranquil waters of financial freedom. This chapter serves as a guide to achieving a harmonious balance, navigating through the serene seas of retirement, wealth preservation, and the fulfillment of life's dreams.

Section A: Finding Serenity in Tranquil Waters

In this chapter, we explore the beauty and tranquility of calm waters and how they provide an opportunity for reflection, rejuvenation, and inner peace. We delve into the importance of finding moments of stillness amidst the busyness of life and the benefits it brings to our overall well-being.

1. Embracing Stillness and Mindfulness

Stillness allows us to quiet the noise within and be fully present in the moment. We discuss the practice of mindfulness and techniques for cultivating stillness in our daily lives. By embracing moments of quiet reflection, we can gain clarity, reduce stress, and connect with our inner selves.

2. Nature's Serenade

The soothing sounds of nature have a profound impact on our well-being. We explore the healing power of nature and the benefits of immersing ourselves in its serenade. Whether it's by the seaside, near a calm lake, or amidst a serene forest, nature offers us a sanctuary to find solace and restore our spirits.

Achieving Financial Freedom

Much like a ship reaching calm waters after navigating turbulent seas, this section explores the concept of financial freedom. Readers delve into strategies for securing a stable financial future, ensuring that the fruits of their labor contribute to a life of comfort and independence. From smart investments to diligent financial planning, the chapter provides insights into achieving a state where financial worries become distant echoes.

Section B: Reflecting on the Journey

In this section, we reflect on the journey we have embarked upon and the lessons we have learned along the way. We contemplate the challenges we have overcome, the growth we have experienced, and the wisdom we have gained.

1. Gratitude for the Voyage

Gratitude is a compass that guides us towards contentment and joy. We discuss the practice of gratitude and its transformative power in shaping our perspective. By expressing gratitude for the voyage we have undertaken, we can acknowledge the blessings, lessons, and experiences that have enriched our lives.

2. Embracing the Winds of Change

Change is an inevitable part of life's journey. We explore the importance of embracing change and the opportunities it presents for growth and transformation. By embracing the winds of change, we can navigate uncharted waters, discover new horizons, and embrace the beauty of the unknown.

Retirement and Wealth Preservation

Retirement is the golden shore that many sailors aspire to reach. This section guides individuals through the considerations and strategies for a fulfilling retirement. Wealth preservation becomes the compass, ensuring that the legacy crafted over a lifetime endures for future generations. Readers gain insights into smart financial practices that secure a legacy while enjoying the serenity of calm financial waters.

As we navigate through Chapter Fourteen, the symbolism of calm waters becomes a metaphor for the reward of disciplined navigation and wise decision-making. The chapter emphasizes that financial freedom is not just a destination but a continuous journey toward a life well-lived.

Section C: Dreaming into the Sunset

The American singer-songwriter Taylor Swift[1] created a song called Calm Waters and Sunset Dreams. It is the tenth album's fourth song Folklore: The Long Pond Studio Sessions, which came out in 2023. The song is a folk-pop tune with acoustic guitar, piano, and harmonica. The words are about being happy and peaceful in a chaotic world, and hoping for a better future with someone you love.

The song got great reviews from music critics, who liked Swift's voice, melody, and emotion. The song was also a big hit, making it to the top ten in many countries, like the US, UK, Canada, and Australia. The song got three Grammy nominations, for Song of the Year, Record of the Year, and Best Pop Solo Performance.

This is part of the song's chorus:

Calm waters and sunset dreams
We're floating on a gentle breeze
We don't need to worry about a thing
We've got each other and that's everything
Calm waters and sunset dreams
We're living in a fantasy
We don't know what tomorrow brings
But we'll face it together, you and me

Calm waters often symbolize serenity and peace. Whether it's a still lake, a gentle river, or a peaceful ocean, the absence of waves and turbulence creates a soothing atmosphere. Calm waters can provide a respite from the chaos and demands of everyday life, offering a space for reflection, relaxation, and rejuvenation. They represent a moment of equilibrium, where the mind can find solace and clarity.

As the sun sets on our journey, we embrace the power of dreams and aspirations. In this section, we explore the significance of dreaming and how it fuels our passion, creativity, and pursuit of a fulfilling life.

1. Vision and Purpose

A compelling vision and sense of purpose propel us towards our dreams. We discuss the importance of clarifying our vision, aligning it with our values, and setting meaningful goals. By connecting with our innermost desires and aspirations, we can pursue a life that is authentic, purposeful, and aligned with our deepest values.

2. Navigating New Horizons

Sunset dreams, on the other hand, evoke a sense of awe and wonder. As the sun descends below the horizon, it paints the sky with a symphony of colors, creating a breathtaking display. The warm hues of orange, pink, and purple cast a magical glow, inviting contemplation and introspection.

Sunsets often symbolize the passage of time, reminding us of the fleeting nature of moments and the beauty that can be found in endings.

Calm waters and sunset dreams have a universal appeal because they tap into our innate longing for peace, beauty, and transcendence. They offer a temporary escape from the complexities and challenges of life, allowing us to reconnect with nature and ourselves. They inspire us to pause, appreciate the present moment, and find solace in the natural world.

Metaphorically, calm waters and sunset dreams can also represent a state of inner peace and contentment. They symbolize a sense of harmony and fulfillment that we strive to achieve in our lives. Just as calm waters reflect a stillness within, sunset dreams can remind us of the importance of chasing our aspirations and embracing the beauty of life's transitions.

As we dream into the sunset, we acknowledge that our journey continues beyond this moment. We explore strategies for navigating new horizons, embracing the unknown, and staying open to the possibilities that lie ahead. By maintaining a sense of adventure and curiosity, we can continue to explore, learn, and grow.

As we bask in the calm waters and sunset dreams, this final chapter reminds us to find moments of stillness, reflect on our journey, and dream into the sunset. By embracing stillness, expressing gratitude, and nurturing our dreams, we can find serenity, fulfillment, and purpose in our lives. So, let us cherish the tranquility of calm waters, gaze into the sunset with hopeful hearts, and embark on new horizons with a sense of wonder and possibility.

In summary, calm waters and sunset dreams evoke a sense of tranquility, beauty, and introspection. They invite us to pause, reflect, and appreciate the simple moments of peace and natural wonders that surround us. Whether in a literal or metaphorical sense, these scenes continue to inspire and captivate, reminding us of the importance of finding moments of stillness and embracing the beauty that exists in both nature and within ourselves.

CHAPTER 15

SAILING INTO THE SUNSET

"We must free ourselves of the hope that the sea will ever rest. We must learn to sail in high winds."
- Aristotle Onassis

Sailing into the sunset is often used as a metaphor for embarking on a new journey, embracing change, and pursuing one's dreams. It evokes a sense of adventure, freedom, and the anticipation of what lies ahead.

When we envision sailing into the sunset, we imagine a scene of serene beauty and tranquility. The sun's warm glow casts vibrant hues across the sky, creating a breathtaking backdrop. The gentle breeze fills the sails, propelling the boat forward, while the sound of the water lapping against the hull creates a soothing rhythm.

In the closing chapters of our odyssey, Chapter Fifteen unfolds as a reflection on the culmination of a life's journey. Much like sailing into the sunset symbolizes the end of a day at sea, this chapter explores the nuances of gracefully concluding one's professional voyage and relishing the rewards of a life well-lived.

Section A: Embracing the Beauty of Closure

In this final chapter, we embrace the beauty of closure and reflect upon the transformative journey we have undertaken. We explore themes of acceptance, letting go, and finding peace as we sail into the sunset.

1. Embracing Closure

Closure allows us to acknowledge and honor the chapters of our lives that have come to an end. We discuss the importance of embracing closure and the healing it brings. By acknowledging the past and finding closure, we create space for new beginnings and personal growth.

2. Letting Go of Attachments

Letting go of attachments is a powerful act of liberation. We delve into the significance of releasing what no longer serves us, whether it be relationships, beliefs, or patterns of behavior. By relinquishing attachments, we open ourselves to new possibilities and create space for personal and spiritual expansion.

Reflecting on the Journey

In this section, we reflect on the profound lessons and insights we have gained throughout our voyage. We contemplate the growth, resilience, and self-discovery that have shaped us into who we are today.

1. Integration and Transformation

Integration is the process of assimilating our experiences and lessons into our being. We explore the importance of reflecting on our journey, acknowledging our growth, and integrating the wisdom we have acquired. By embracing the transformative power of our experiences, we can cultivate resilience and continue evolving.

2. Celebrating Milestones and Achievements

As we sail into the sunset, we celebrate the milestones and achievements that have marked our journey. We discuss the significance of recognizing our accomplishments, both big and small, and the joy that comes from celebrating our progress. By acknowledging our achievements, we cultivate a sense of fulfillment and gratitude.

As sailors approach the sunset of their careers, reflection becomes a crucial aspect of the voyage. This section encourages individuals to look back on their journey, acknowledging milestones, learning from challenges, and celebrating achievements. Through personal stories, readers gain insights into the power of introspection as a tool for personal and professional growth.

Metaphorically, sailing into the sunset represents the pursuit of new experiences, personal growth, and the courage to leave behind the familiar. It symbolizes a willingness to venture into the unknown, face challenges, and embrace the possibilities that lie beyond the horizon. It embodies the spirit of exploration, discovery, and the desire to carve out one's own path in life.

Section B: Embracing the Eternal Voyage
In this final section, we embrace the notion that while one voyage may end, the eternal voyage of personal growth and

self-discovery continues. We explore the importance of nurturing a lifelong commitment to learning, growth, and self-reflection.

1. Lifelong Learning and Curiosity

Lifelong learning is the compass that guides us on our eternal voyage. We discuss the significance of cultivating curiosity, embracing new experiences, and pursuing knowledge. By remaining open to learning, we continue to expand our horizons and embrace the richness of life.

2. Embracing the Unknown

As we sail into the sunset, we embrace the beauty of the unknown. We discuss the importance of embracing uncertainty, taking risks, and trusting in the journey ahead. By embracing the unknown, we step into a world of endless possibilities and continue to evolve into our highest selves.

Sailing into the sunset also carries a sense of optimism and hope. It signifies the belief that each journey has the potential for a positive outcome, even if the destination is uncertain. It reminds us that life is a continuous voyage, and the act of sailing into the sunset represents a willingness to keep moving forward, regardless of the obstacles encountered along the way.

Furthermore, sailing into the sunset can be seen as a metaphor for letting go of the past and embracing a new chapter. Just as the sun sets, signaling the end of one day, sailing into the sunset can symbolize leaving behind old patterns, regrets, or limitations, and embracing a fresh start. It encourages us to release what no longer serves us and embark on a journey of self-discovery, growth, and fulfillment.

As we sail into the sunset, this final chapter encourages us to embrace closure, let go of attachments, reflect on our journey, and continue embracing the eternal voyage of growth and self-discovery. By finding peace in closure, celebrating our achievements, and nurturing a commitment to lifelong learning, we embark on a journey of infinite potential and fulfillment. So, let us set sail into the sunset, guided by the wisdom gained and the spirit of adventure in our hearts, knowing that the voyage of self-discovery continues to unfold, evermore beautiful and profound.

Section C : Summing Up Millionaires Offshore

The chapter culminates by summarizing the key themes and lessons explored throughout "Millionaires Offshore." From the early struggles faced in Chapter One to the reflections on legacy in Chapter Twelve, readers are reminded of the transformative journey undertaken. This section serves as a compass, guiding individuals to distill the wisdom gained and apply it to their ongoing and future ventures.

Chapter Fifteen serve as a sunset on a well-navigated voyage, allowing you to appreciate the vast sea of experiences, triumphs, and lessons learned throughout your journey. As you sail into the sunset, may the horizon ahead be filled with the promise of new beginnings and the fulfillment of dreams.

In summary, sailing into the sunset is a powerful metaphor that embodies the spirit of adventure, personal growth, and embracing the unknown. It represents the courage to pursue dreams, explore new horizons, and let go of the past. Whether taken literally or figuratively, sailing into the sunset invites us to embark on a journey of self-discovery, optimism, and the pursuit of a life filled with meaning and fulfillment.

CHAPTER 16

CONCLUSION

"If you want something new, you have to stop doing something old."

- Peter F. Drucker

In the final chapter of "Millionaires Offshore:Blueprint of Success," our journey comes full circle. This concluding chapter encapsulates the essence of the odyssey, offering reflections, encouragement, and a call to action as readers prepare to chart their own courses.

Section A: Reflections on the Journey

As we stand at the helm of our reflections, we acknowledge the challenges faced, the triumphs celebrated, and the invaluable lessons learned. This section prompts readers to pause and consider the transformative nature of their personal odyssey, encouraging introspection on the wisdom gained from the turbulent seas of life.

Section B: Encouragement for Readers to Chart Their Own Course

The conclusion is not just an end but a commencement. This section serves as a compass for readers embarking on their own journeys, encouraging them to apply the insights gained from "Millionaires Offshore." Whether setting sail in the realms of entrepreneurship, wealth-building, or personal growth, readers are inspired to harness the winds of wisdom as they navigate their unique waters.

As we conclude our narrative, dear reader, may the tales shared in "Millionaires Offshore" linger in your thoughts like the echoes of the sea. May the lessons learned be the stars guiding you through the uncharted skies of your future endeavors. As you embark on your own voyage, may you find inspiration, resilience, and the courage to set sail into the vast expanse of possibilities that await.

CHAPTER 17

FINAL THOUGHTS

"Every moment and every event of every man's life on earth plants something in his soul."
- Thomas Merton

As we reach the shore of our conversation, I hope the journey through the chapters of "Millionaires Offshore" has been insightful and inspiring. Life, much like the sea, is filled with unpredictable currents, but your ability to navigate challenges, set ambitious goals, and embrace innovation can lead to a fulfilling and prosperous voyage.

Remember, the lessons learned from others' journeys are compass points, not predetermined routes. Your unique path awaits, and with the wisdom gained, may you set sail confidently into the future, crafting your own narrative of success.

If there are specific areas or questions you'd like to explore further, feel free to let me know. Bon voyage on your personal odyssey!

GLOSSARY

1. Adaptability: The ability to adjust and thrive in changing or challenging conditions.

2. Alternative Investments: Non-traditional investment opportunities beyond stocks and bonds.

3. Anchor: A metaphorical representation of stability or a secure foundation in life.

4. Archipelago: A metaphor for building a diversified and resilient network of investments or achievements.

5. Calm Waters: A metaphor for stability, tranquility, and financial comfort.

6. Casting Off: The symbolic act of releasing oneself from the moorings of fear, doubt, and societal expectations to begin a transformative journey.

7. Complacency: A state of self-satisfaction that may lead to stagnation or a lack of progress.

8. Courage: The ability to confront fear, adversity, or challenges with bravery and determination.

9. Digital Transformation: The integration of digital technology into various aspects of business or life.

10. Diversification: Spreading investments or efforts across various areas to reduce risk.

11. Entrepreneurship: The process of starting and operating a business, often involving innovation and risk-taking.

12. Epiphany: A sudden realization or understanding that brings clarity and insight.

13. Financial Archipelago: A metaphorical representation of a well-diversified and stable financial portfolio.

14. Financial Freedom: The state of having enough financial resources to live comfortably and make choices without constraints.

15. Financial Portfolio: A collection of financial assets such as stocks, bonds, and investments.

16. Global Perspectives: A broad and inclusive viewpoint that considers international or worldwide factors.

17. Horizon: The line at which the Earth's surface and the sky appear to meet, often symbolizing the future or potential.

18. Innovation: The introduction of new ideas, methods, or products to create positive change.

19. Inspirational Quotes: Powerful and motivational statements from notable individuals.

20. Introspection: Reflecting on one's own thoughts, feelings, and motivations.

21. Legacy: The impact or contributions one leaves behind, often beyond personal success.

22. Legacy Building: The intentional creation of a lasting impact or contribution to society.

23. Leadership: The ability to guide and influence others towards achieving common goals.

24. Mentorship: Guidance and support provided by an experienced and knowledgeable mentor.

25. Navigating: The process of planning and directing a course, often through challenges or opportunities.

26. Navigational Compass: A tool or metaphorical guide used to find direction and make decisions.

27. North Star: A metaphorical guiding principle or goal that provides direction and purpose in one's journey.

28. Odyssey: A long and eventful journey marked by various experiences and adventures.

29. Organizational Leadership: Leading a group or company towards a shared vision and goals.

30. Philanthropy: The act of contributing time, resources, or efforts for the well-being of others or the community.

31. Pioneering Paths: Charting new courses or approaches in a particular field or endeavor.

32. Purpose: The reason for which something is done or created, often serving as a motivating force.

33. Real Estate: Property, land, or buildings, often considered as an investment.

34. Recalibration: Adjusting or realigning one's goals, plans, or strategies based on changing circumstances.

35. Resilience: The ability to bounce back from challenges, setbacks, or adversity.

36. Retirement: The period in life when one stops working and typically relies on accumulated savings.

37. Risk and Reward: The balance between the potential for gain and the level of risk involved in a decision or action.

38. Sailor: An individual navigating the seas of life, facing challenges and seeking opportunities.

39. Sunset Dreams: A symbol of fulfillment, contentment, and achieving life's aspirations.

40. Success: The achievement of goals, objectives, or a desired outcome.

41. Societal Challenges: Issues or obstacles arising from

cultural, social, or community norms.

42. Stock Market: A marketplace where shares of publicly held companies are bought and sold.

43. Tranquil: Calm, serene, and free from disturbance.

44. Transformative Power: The capacity to bring about significant positive change or evolution.

45. Undulating Tides: The natural rise and fall of circumstances or emotions in life.

46. Uncharted Waters: Areas or aspects of life that are unknown, unpredictable, and have not been explored.

47. Vision: A clear and inspiring mental image of the desired future state.

48. Wealth Preservation: Strategies and practices to protect and maintain accumulated wealth.

49. Alternative Investments: Non-traditional investment opportunities beyond stocks and bonds.

50. Continuous Process: An ongoing and evolving series of actions or steps.

REFERENCE

(1) What is the North Star and How Do You Find It? - NASA Science. https://science.nasa.gov/solar-system/skywatching/what-is-the-north-star-and-how-do-you-find-it/.

(2) 3 Ways to Find the North Star - wikiHow. https://www.wikihow.com/Find-the-North-Star.

(3) How to find the North Star - BBC Sky at Night Magazine. https://www.skyatnightmagazine.com/advice/skills/how-find-polaris-north-star.

(4) Leading differently in a changing global landscape | World Economic Forum. https://www.weforum.org/agenda/2022/06/young-global-leaders-lead-differently-changing-global-landscape/.

(5) Four Scenarios for Geopolitical Order in 2025-2030: What Will Great .... https://www.csis.org/analysis/four-scenarios-geopolitical-order-2025-2030-what-will-great-power-competition-look.

(6) Landscape dynamics determine the evolution of ... - ScienceDaily. https://www.sciencedaily.com/releases/2023/11/231129112401.htm.

(7) Most detailed geological model reveals Earth's past 100 million years. https://phys.org/news/2023-02-geological-reveals-earth-million-years.html.

(8) The most successful Entrepreneurs in Nigeria (2024). https://www.makemoney.ng/the-most-successful-entrepreneurs-in-nigeria/.

(9) Top 10 most influential entrepreneurs in Nigeria - Vanguard News. https://www.vanguardngr.com/2020/11/top-10-most-influential-entrepreneurs-in-nigeria/.

(10) List of Nigerian entrepreneurs - Wikipedia. https://en.wikipedia.org/wiki/List_of_Nigerian_entrepreneurs.

(11) 75 of the Most Epic and Inspirational Sailing Quotes - Navigate Content. https://www.navigatecontent.com/sailing-adventure-blog/epic-and-inspirational-sailing-quotes.

(12) The 79 Most Inspiring Sailing Quotes - Two Get Lost. https://twogetlost.com/the-79-most-inspiring-sailing-quotes.

(13) The 74 Best Sailing Quotes. https://www.deepsailing.com/blog/sailing-quotes.

(14) Tunde Ednut Biography, Age, Early Life, Family, Education, Career And .... https://www.infoguideafrica.com/2021/01/tunde-ednut-biography.html.

(15) Tunde Ednut - Wikipedia. https://en.wikipedia.org/wiki/Tunde_Ednut.

(16) Decoding Tunde Ednut's biography: age, height, real name, net worth .... https://www.legit.ng/1398646-tunde-ednut-biography-age-height-real-net-worth-songs.html.

(17) A Complete Timeline Of Steve Rogers And The Legacy Of The Captain .... https://www.ranker.com/list/captain-america-mcu-timeline/stephanroget.

(18) Captain Sir Tom Moore: What has happened to his legacy? - BBC. https://www.bbc.com/news/uk-england-beds-bucks-herts-66134840.

(19) Captain Tom: Inside the village facing the 'tarnished legacy' of .... https://www.independent.co.uk/news/uk/home-news/captain-tom-spa-marston-moretaine-nhs-b2485353.html.

(20) Raising the sail of innovation: Philosophical explorations on .... https://research.wur.nl/en/publications/raising-the-sail-of-innovation-philosophical-explorations-on-resp.

(21) Raising the sail of innovation - Academia.edu. https://www.academia.edu/110574977/Raising_the_sail_of_innovation_Philosophical_explorations_on_responsible_innovation.

(22) Lucien Schomberg, Raising the sail of innovation - PhilPapers. https://philpapers.org/rec/SCHRTS-11.

(23) undefined. https://doi.org/10.18174/560519.

(24) Climate and weather related disasters surge five-fold over 50 years .... https://news.un.org/en/story/2021/09/1098662.

(25) There are 4 economic scenarios for the rest of the decade: I've .... https://theconversation.com/there-are-4-economic-scenarios-for-the-rest-of-the-decade-ive-reluctantly-picked-one-217519.

(26) Weathering the Storm in Times of Economic Uncertainty. https://medium.com/@bettercallron__/weathering-the-storm-in-times-of-economic-uncertainty-cac059a58ca2.

(27) A New Look at the Effects of Weather Shocks Over Time. https://www.richmondfed.org/publications/research/economic_brief/2023/eb_23-25.

(28) Loan Officer Hub blog. https://loanofficerhub.com/en/blog/3-secrets-to-surviving-an-economic-storm.

(29) Deep Calming Sleep Music - Sunset Dream-state - YouTube.

https://www.youtube.com/watch?v=aG4tB0kkVo0.

(30) The Deep Meaning of Sunset Dreams – (With Scenarios) - Symbol Sage. https://symbolsage.com/dreaming-of-sunsets-meaning/.

(31) 25 Ocean Dream Meaning and Interpretations | Sarah Scoop. https://sarahscoop.com/ocean-dream-meaning/.

ABOUT THE AUTHOR

Akinwunmi Oyedola Dosumu is a teacher and entrepreneur navigating the seas of success from the vibrant city of Abuja, Nigeria. With a passion for innovation, wealth creation, and global perspectives, Akinwunmi has not only built a prosperous financial portfolio but has also contributed to the economic landscape in impactful ways.

As a seasoned navigator of the business world, his journey has been marked by resilience, strategic decision-making, and a commitment to continuous growth. His ventures have not only flourished on the local stage but have also set sail into the international waters, harnessing the potential of offshore opportunities.

Beyond the realm of entrepreneurship, Akinwunmi is recognized for his philanthropic endeavors, shaping a legacy that extends beyond financial success. His commitment to giving back to the community and contributing to societal well-being reflects a holistic approach to wealth and success.

In the pages of "Millionaires Offshore," Akinwunmi Oyedola Dosumu shares not only his personal narrative but also the wisdom gained from the diverse stories of successful individuals navigating the vast seas of life.

May this journey inspire you, the reader, to chart your own course towards prosperity, innovation, and a life well-lived.